Praise for

"I enjoyed reading *Diary of a Country Mother*, and learning about Tim's effect on so many people. This book attests to the fact that each and every person, regardless of any limitations or ailments, has profound value and can have significant impact on the lives of those around them."

—Most Reverend Henry J. Mansell,
Archbishop of Hartford, Connecticut

"*Diary of a Country Mother* is an inspiring narrative about the redeemed sufferings of a mentally disturbed child with a beautiful soul. As we read this blend of Scripture, quotations from holy people, and the thoughts of Tim's mother, we become reconciled to our own sufferings."

—Ronda Chervin, Ph.D, *The Kiss from the Cross;
Saints for Every Kind of Suffering*

"As I turned the pages I was drawn in, not to a tragedy but to the life of a family immersed in the beauty of a faith-filled life. Cynthia Montanaro's memoir is painted against the backdrop of a full year in the New England countryside where the daily pattern of a sacramental life, close to God and to the earth, brings healing, peace, and wisdom. *Diary of a Country Mother* gives me hope that I too, will be sustained by grace in life's darkest moments."

—Daria Sockey, *Everyday Catholic's Guide
to the Liturgy of the Hours*

"What an honor and blessing to read this gently flowing memoir about Timothy, a young man who mysteriously and tragically left this world while still a youth. Yet thanks to his devoted mother, his life and death now serve to remind each of us that all hope is possible in the firmness of faith and the merciful love of Our Lord, Jesus Christ."

—Patricia Hershwitzky, founder of Trinity Bridge

"I love Cynthia's friendly, down to earth style. Her strong faith is warmly wrapped around each day, offering precious comfort and hope to grievers who have faced similar circumstances. Families who have dealt with ADHD or Tourette Syndrome will find validation and strength in Diary of a Country Mother."

—Elaine Stillwell, *The Death of a Child, Reflections for Grieving Parents*

"I laughed, I cried, I prayed, I thanked God for the opportunity to meet Tim and to know such a devoted family. God bless a Country Mother who taught this city girl how much more to love my kids."

—Lynda Collins, homeschooling mother

"Like Our Lady's grief at the death of her Son, Cynthia's sorrow is illuminated and shot through by the light of the resurrected Christ. Consequently, this book is in no way depressing. Instead, it records the peace that passes understanding, the confident hope that true faith gives, and above all, love elevated and fulfilled by Love. The reader will come to know Tim well, and to know him is absolutely to love him."

—Suzie Andres, *A Little Way of Homeschooling*

Diary of a Country Mother

Diary of a Country Mother

A Year Remembering Tim

by
Cynthia A. Montanaro

Photographs by Andrew M. Montanaro

Roman Catholic Books
Fort Collins, Colorado

Copyright © 2013 Cynthia A. Montanaro

Printed in the United States of America

All rights reserved

Cover design by Ted Schluenderfritz

Interior design by Nora Malone

No part of this book may be reproduced, stored in a retrieval system, or transmitted in any form, or by any means, electronic, mechanical, photocopying, or otherwise, without the prior written permission of the publisher, except by a reviewer, who may quote brief passages in a review.

Permission has been granted from Scepter Publishers to quote passages from Fr. Francis Fernandez and St. Josemaria Escriva.

Roman Catholic Books
P. O. Box 2286, Fort Collins, Colorado 80522
BooksforCatholics.com

ISBN 978-1-934888-33-9

To Mary, our Mother in the far country
who now has the pleasure of watching over Tim
and to all Tim's family here below

May we all live well with God's strength,
so with Tim
"when the busy world is hushed"
we can enjoy
"a safe lodging and a holy rest
and peace at the last"

Contents

Introduction. ix
December 3
January. 15
February. 35
March 51
April 69
May. 89
June 101
July 127
August 145
September. 167
October 191
November. 207
December 227

Conversations. 239

Introduction

Five years ago today I picked up my pen and started a year-long journey of prayer, meditation, and writing. I envisioned an extended period of time in which to record, before memory failed me, all of the little humorous and profound incidents that made up my son Tim's short life. As God guided me along the way I discovered new meanings in the ordinary play of events and uncovered God's hand at every step and around every corner. I also found a deep and lasting peace and, yes, a great joy as I contemplated the big picture.

Tim's death in June of 2005 was totally unexpected. His early diagnosis of Tourette Syndrome with accompanying phobias and obsessive compulsive tendencies had led us on a roller coaster ride over the years. It had been a wild ride we could never have imagined, with difficulties that made life worrisome on the steep climb up the grade. But through it all we had Tim's laughter and glee as we held hands and screamed on the speeding downward track.

What my husband Andy and I never expected was the brick wall Tim smashed into at the end. There were no warning lights or signs of imminent danger. Tim never articulated his obsessive thoughts, could never put his fears into words.

I do not imagine he had any idea that his actions would result in the finality of death. I view his last compulsive act as an unpremeditated action that ultimately had a tragic ending. An unpremeditated action is "spontaneous, impulsive and will-less," according to Webster, and that was Tim to a tee.

This diary is not the anatomy of an illness, though, or a treatise on mental disorders. It is not a blueprint to prevent tragedy. I am not the person to write that book. This account of the life of my son simply reveals that each person, no matter his mental or physical problems, has a great worth beyond measure and leaves an enormous impact on those near to them and on those farther afield.

For those of you who never had a chance to meet Tim or come to know him well, I am delighted to introduce you. One of the great joys of his life was meeting new people, and unlike his introverted parents he had no qualms about approaching anyone, anywhere, anytime.

INTRODUCTION

It gives me great pleasure, then, to present Timothy Andrew Zozimus Montanaro, the boy with the big smile and the even bigger heart.

December 8, 2010
The Immaculate Conception

O how everything that is suffered with love is healed again.

—St. Teresa of Avila

Diary of a Country Mother

December

December 8, 2005

Yesterday was one of those milestone days that mark the passage through life, and I was determined to put aside some time and begin writing but the circumstances of my day dictated otherwise. So today, on the feast of the Immaculate Conception, I begin to pour out the memories of Tim that I have so guarded over the past six months. Half a year ago Tim died. I can't fathom the thought still. I can't believe it has been so long that I have been without his man-sized hug and his unforgettable personality. I don't know how I will continue without him to fill my days, but fill them I must.

I have been thinking of Tim a lot in the months since his death. I guess that is only natural. I remember things he did or said and they all are replayed with a new significance.

Ever since Timothy was a small boy, I have been recording the little incidents or conversations that took place in the course of a day. He was such an unusual child and his way of thinking and expressing himself was priceless. I had in mind, as the years passed, to write a book someday about our life with Tim. I wanted to wait, I told myself, to see where Tim's life would lead him before beginning the story. And now the ending has come with no warning and no time for preparation.

One day, about a year ago, as I recorded one of my conversations with Tim, he asked me what I was doing. I told him about the journal I had been keeping and about my plans for future writing. Around this time the Adult Discussion Group at our parish had been reading *The Diary of a Country Priest* by Georges Bernanos, and Tim had been watching me make posters and flyers. With this fresh in his mind, he said, "I know, Mom . . . you could call it the *Diary of a Country Mother*!"

This is Tim's book. He has provided the material and the title, and his death has now given me the opportunity and the time to relate the joy that I have in remembering him.

December 11, 2005

It is a still Sunday morning and from where I sit I can see the beginning of a sunrise over the distant hills. On Friday we had our first significant snowfall of the year and now over a foot of powder lies atop the brown fall landscape. It is wonderfully beautiful and I offer my Te Deum to the Author of beauty.

Last night Andy and I watched the last twenty minutes of George Bailey's frantic rush around Bedford Falls, glimpsing what it would have meant to those in his family and his town had he never lived, the classic scene from "It's a Wonderful Life." In the final frames we see a grateful and ecstatic George surrounded by his family and neighbors, overwhelmed with their generosity and love as Christmas carols are tearfully sung.

As I woke this morning and remembered the scene, my thoughts flew to Tim and to my reasons for writing this remembrance of him. It has a lot to do with celebrating the impact of one soul on those around him, providing a "ratio" for his existence. I feel this compelling need for explanation to the world, to his acquaintances, to his family and especially to those who suffer under the weight of feelings of worthlessness. I almost feel as if I am writing it for Tim himself who had, in the last several years of his fifteen, wondered about his place in the world.

"I know God is all powerful and can't make mistakes, but I think He made a mistake when he made me," we heard Tim say a number of times. Now, however, Tim needs no explanations or expositions. His immortal soul has received the true knowledge from his Father God of his special place in creation, and he is at peace.

No, this memory of Tim is for a time and a world that measures the worth of people in their quality of life, in their perfection of body and fitness of mind. It is for a world that all too often discards its young ones at the first inkling of disease or malformation. It is for Tim's adopted friends so they might treasure their place within their families; it is for his friends with mental illness so they, too, might value the life God has given them.

I write for myself, as well, for I want to hold Tim close in my mind just a little longer. I want to remember and record before the thoughts slip away and the mementoes of our days together are buried with other thoughts and experiences. I write for my husband, Andy, and for Tim's brothers who gained so much by his presence and who now must live without him.

Over and above all, this is a thanksgiving journal to God, the Author of Life and the giver of every good gift. It IS a wonderful life, Tim!

> *I will give thanks to the Lord with all my heart*
> *In the company and assembly of the just.*
> *Great are the works of the Lord,*
> *Exquisite in all their delights.*

—Psalm 11:1-2

December 17, 2005, Morning

Another dawn is rolling slowly over the hills on a frosty morning. I sit inside with a cup of hot tea and take advantage of the morning quiet to write.

In a little while Andy and I will dress and brave the cold and make our way down the Blandford hills and along the Westfield River to the little town of Huntington for morning Mass. Our godson Mark is with us so we will have his red-haired, five-year-old liveliness along to brighten the ride. Today is the anniversary of Tim's baptism, and we will head for church and the presence of God to offer our gratitude for his life and the gifts of grace he was given along the way. We will pass the cemetery as we drive. Another bittersweet day.

The sweetness is there, though. It is in the light of the sunrise and the remembering hearts. A large measure of that sweet peace is due to the faith we have that Tim's story has a happy ending and an ending that has no end. Due to his learning disabilities, we spent a lot of time reading to Timothy. He loved books that had sequels; he didn't want the story to end. When he was little we read the *Little House on the Prairie* books and as the years went by, the *Chronicles of Narnia* and Tolkien's *Lord of the Rings* trilogy. There was always more to come.

Now Tim is *in* the never-ending story! Eternity means always one more chapter, and the story comes from the best book ever conceived. How marvelous! And how nearly impossible for the human mind to comprehend. All the memories we have of perfect days are of days that had a natural end. The sun sets, we say our farewells, put out the lights, and we go to sleep.

Our perfect certitude that Tim now experiences eternity comes in large measure from the grace he received on the day we celebrate today.

He was baptized in a beautiful sanctuary in Cranston, Rhode Island. It was dedicated to Our Lady under the title of *Madonna de la Civita*, a copy of a church in Italy held dear in memory by the Italian immigrants of the neighborhood. Tim was still a tiny babe, a day shy of one month old, and Andy and I had petitioned for his early baptism. We didn't want to wait until the adoption was finalized, which could take about a year. With our eyes on eternity, we dressed Timothy Andrew in the family baptismal gown worn by his brothers at their baptisms, with his name embroidered along with theirs on the hem of the slip. We invited family and friends to witness the adoption by God of a new child of His. We dedicated this new child of eternity to the Mother of God after the baptismal rites and then we celebrated. As we do today.

Afternoon

At Mass this morning, when the deacon read the Gospel, we heard the genealogy of Christ. In his homily our pastor referred to the ancients' interest in genealogy and to the resurgence in genealogical research in our own day. He pointed out, though, that the only genealogy that has any lasting value is that which is ours by virtue of our baptism. We have been adopted into the family of God and by His death and resurrection we have a right to our portion of a son's inheritance: Eternal Life.

I sat and listened and smiled inwardly at another instance of God's eternal watchfulness. We were here to celebrate Tim's baptism, and we heard the words that would best console and inspire us. It was indeed another day to celebrate.

After Mass, Mark marveled at the donkey and sheep and calves in the living nativity outside of church, much as Tim would have done even at fifteen, and then we headed back past the cemetery and on to pick out our Christmas tree. There was a thick layer of ice atop the snow and our footfalls crunched as we inspected the trees and Mark helped cut the chosen one.

We remember, we celebrate and we give thanks.

Each child that is born brings to us the smile of God and invites us to recognize that life is His gift, a gift that must be accepted with love and protected with care, always and at all times . . . Baptism is adoption into the family of God, in communion with the Holy Trinity.

> —Pope Benedict XVI, Sistine Chapel Baptisms
> 7 January 2007, Baptism of the Lord

"I guess God adopted all the people just like you guys adopted me."

—Tim

January

January 2, 2006

The past weeks have sped by, filled with Christmas preparations and family visits. Joy has been in the forefront with only small cracks for the sadness to seep through. Thoughts of Timothy have been in my decorating and baking; remembering his boundless enthusiasm for all holidays, but especially Christmas.

I have also had hundreds of images of Tim pass through my hands as I sorted the family photographs that we have amassed over the years. Yes, amassed is the right word. With a husband whose avocation is photography, there are albums and boxes of photos everywhere, and Tim was always a convenient and willing subject. There were enough pictures of him to fill three large albums for his brothers, two for the grandparents and an even larger album for Andy and me. The photos show him climbing, running, swimming, posing and hugging, often with arms stretched wide and a smile to match. To look at them brings enormous joy

that only grows when we recall the person Tim was at each click of the shutter.

After I had begun the hunting and sorting of images this summer, I came across a quote from Blessed John XXIII:

"Oh, the joy of that moment when we shall all meet in heaven, and there will be no more need of photographs, because we shall see each other in the Lord's light forever."

It seems to put a fitting perspective onto our family's and our culture's need to preserve moments in time with

images. The pictures are precious to us now because we need their consolation, but we live in hope for the day when the Lord's light will illumine every one of our moments and reunite us all in love.

January 4, 2006

Another sunrise competes with the twinkle of lights on the Christmas tree, artificial light and natural light combining to brighten our darkened world. In the quiet morning I look back over the Christmas festivities, aglow with laughter and small voices as our son Matthew and his family arrived from Alabama. It was a joy to have the house filled with children again. His boys so closely resemble our own boys at that age both in appearance and temperament that their presence brings the past to my mind.

In order to convey Tim's impact on our family, I need to describe that point in our history when Tim first entered our lives. The scenes of Christmas with our grandchildren are set aside, and my memory turns to even earlier days.

Andy and I met in California in the 1970's, during our years at Thomas Aquinas College. As our friendship developed, we had long talks on philosophy, theology, and a host of other topics, and came to know and to love each other and to recognize that marriage was our mutual vocation. We also shared a job at a local ranch and traveled back and forth twice a day to feed the cattle and horses; during these trips we touched on our hopes for a simple country life that would include lots of children and a variety of animals. Lack of money being the ever-present factor in our plans, we decided to leave college so Andy could begin the job search and I could work and plan for the wedding.

We were married in St. Louis, Missouri at the Old Cathedral on the banks of the Mississippi River, the Basilica of St. Louis, King of France, and began our married life in Syracuse, New York. Our first two sons, Matthew and Thomas, were born during our years in Syracuse and then after a move to Utica, New York, Paul joined our little family. Before his first birthday, however, we received bad news. During a routine chest x-ray at the hospital where he worked, Andy was diagnosed with Hodgkin's Disease—cancer of the lymph system. Surgery and chemotherapy followed, and Andy suffered greatly as I struggled to help him and keep the house running while caring for two preschoolers and a baby.

Thanks to the grace of God and the prayers of family and friends, Andy progressed well and gradually regained his strength. The chances that we would have any more children, however, were dubious. We put our future in God's hands and gave thanks to Him for returning Andy to our family circle.

The following years saw us moving again to Cohoes, New York and then to Cranston, Rhode Island. The boys were growing up, but no brothers or sisters had come along. We were persistent in prayer for this intention, and the boys added their pleas to ours. Paul was especially intent in his prayers for a younger sibling.

In Cranston we continued our homeschooling, and I became a member of a Legion of Mary Praesidium that had a pro-life apostolate. My duties included answering weekend calls for a Problem Pregnancy hot line and serving as a board member of the Little Flower Home for pregnant teens and women. Andy and I talked about adopting a baby.

That's when the next blow came. Paul's headaches and nausea were not due to a persistent flu but to a brain tumor. After his diagnosis on Good Friday, he received the Anointing of the Sick and his First Communion on Holy Saturday, and then a week later he underwent surgery to remove the tumor. We suffered to see our dear seven-year-old go through the agony of a seven hour operation and weeks of recovery, but once again we threw ourselves on the mercy of God and begged prayers from everyone. In time Paul recovered, and we renewed our prayers of gratitude that our family was still intact.

It was now the summer of 1989, and we had just arrived home from a vacation in California where we had gone to attend a family wedding. The boys had never flown before, and the Pacific Ocean and Disneyland rounded out the excitement for them. At twelve, eleven, and nine, our sons were great company, but there was still that longing in our hearts for another child. Then came the phone call that would change the pattern of our lives forever. One of the residents of the Little Flower Home was expecting a baby in December and looking for an adoptive family for her child.

> *His own designs shall stand forever,*
> *The plans of his heart from age to age.*
>
> —Psalm 33: 11

January 7, 2006
Bath, PA

This evening we gathered at my brother Michael's house and sang Christmas carols to usher in the feast of the Epiphany. We began with "We Three Kings" and ended with "Away in a Manger" as a lullaby for a sleepy three-year-old Margaret. We sang about the kings setting their gifts before the Christ Child, each gift chosen with particular regard for its eternal significance. Later, when the house was all abed, I began to think about the nature of gifts, especially those which have an everlasting meaning. I can see the birth announcement we sent out with our Christmas cards in 1989. I had stenciled a holly leaf around the verse from the letter of James proclaiming, "Every good and perfect gift is from above, coming down from the Father of lights."

We had prayed for a child and considered the birth of Timothy God's perfect gift in answer to our prayer. That he came as an adopted child did not lessen the gift in any way. We celebrated his first Christmas with that inexpressible thanksgiving that all mothers and fathers feel when cradling an infant in their arms.

Our sons had been hoping for another brother, and each showed his acceptance and joy in his own way. Matthew splurged with money saved from his paper route and took us all out for dinner. Tom and Paul offered names for the baby, and together we peered through the nursery windows to catch a glimpse of the newest addition to our family.

A year later on January 7, 1990, the entire family assembled at the court house in Providence for Tim's final adoption ceremony. With a squirming one-year-old and proud grandparents, in our Sunday best we presented ourselves before the judge, who happily formalized Tim's acceptance into the Montanaro family. I remember thinking that it must be a pleasant turn of events for a judge to preside at an

adoption as opposed to the scores of other more sordid court proceedings. Papers were signed and filed, and we went home to celebrate. The menu was pizza and eggnog, favorites of the guest of honor.

So every January 7th we repeat the menu as we celebrate Timothy's "Adoption Day." I couldn't find the eggnog this year, but I made the pizza for my nieces and nephews in Tim's honor and we toasted him with root beer and ginger ale. This year we rejoice in the consolation of the Holy Spirit who fills us with Divine Love and in thanksgiving for our "good and perfect gift."

JANUARY

Only God knows the gifts that are best for us. We spend countless hours searching out and shopping for gifts that will delight only to later spend countless hours in line exchanging the presents that weren't just right after all. We fail miserably to gauge the desires of others.

In our prayers we often petition God for gifts that do not fit us or are not really worthy of desire. In His infinite goodness God overlooks our feeble attempts and rewards the faithful prayer with made-to-order answers. Tim was just such a gift for our family. His arrival was perfectly timed and, with the omnipotent knowledge of the Giver, all was arranged so that our previous attempts at adopting fell through, but this particular child found his way home to us.

As he grew older, we explained "Adoption Day" to Tim in language that he could understand. We gave him his own picture album and retold the story again and again over pizza and eggnog. His response was always as big-hearted and filled with enthusiasm as was Tim himself. He wanted to share the family and the love he had been given. He prayed that God would rain down orphans from the sky onto our house and then we would catch them with big umbrellas. His primary job would be to play with them. Mom and sister-in-law Anya could change diapers. His solution for older homeless children involved us leaving the light on outside so if any orphans were wandering around they would know whose house to come to.

Each person is a reflection of the Creator, or in the words we learned as young ones, "We are made in the image and likeness of God." I like to think that Tim mirrors that big-hearted love of God for each one of us, a God whose gifts of love, beginning with the gift of His only-begotten Son, are each one so marvelous and well-fitting and eternally priceless.

> *As they offered gifts most rare*
> *At that manger rude and bare,*
> *So may we with holy joy,*
> *Pure and free from sin's alloy,*
> *All our costliest treasures bring,*
> *Christ, to thee our heavenly king.*
>
> —W. Chesterton Dix
> "As with Gladness Men of Old"

༄

January 16, 2006

The weather has turned frigid again after a week of mildness and thawing and the ever-present mud. Mud is an inevitable feature of life in rural New England when you live on a dirt road. The fickle weather has postponed that problem, though, for snow has covered the mud again, and Andy and I have been out with our shovels to clear some paths.

Later, I gazed out over the back acres and watched the wind whipping down the small inclines, constantly re-arranging the piles of snow. Sometimes the snow would fly down in sheets and the next moment it would spin around in miniature funnels. This sparked a memory of Tim lying on the school room bed and watching the wind streak across the top of the deep snow. His interest was concentrated on the changing scene before him and he had to be brought back at periodic intervals to the task he was struggling to complete.

Tim had an infectious sense of wonder and enthusiasm that remained with him all his life but was especially pronounced and endearing in his middle years. Often the wonder was directed at the world of natural beauty around him: a gorgeous sunset, a large expanse of water, an enormous tree, the million pin-points of stars that brilliantly light up our country skies, a tiny kitten. I think of this wonder as infectious because it immediately telegraphed itself to those near enough to feel the spark and produced in them a like response. It was a most amazing and beautiful thing to witness!

For we do live in a world that is overflowing with landscapes of beauty and physical features that should stop us dead in our tracks for their sheer size or arrangement or perfection of design. The really sad thing is that we often overlook the wonderful because it is always before us. Tim's enthusiasm was a constant reminder of our need to wonder anew at each marvel. His attitude reminded us also to take it one step further, as we had taught him but ourselves too easily forgot, and contemplate the Author of our world of wonders, rendering homage and thanks for the visual expression of His love for us and for the glimpse it gives us of His awesome nature.

So now I can't watch the whirling snow or glimpse the sunrise unfold or catch the colors of a rainbow in the clouds or see the fog creeping over the ocean swells without feeling Tim at my side and sensing his response and praising the God of wonders. And it is good.

> *We sing the mighty power of God*
> *That made the mountains rise,*
> *That spread the flowing seas abroad*
> *And built the lofty skies.*
> *We sing the wisdom that ordained*
> *The sun to rule the day;*

JANUARY

*The moon shines full at God's command
And all the stars obey!*

—Isaac Watts
"We Sing the Mighty Power of God"

January 23, 2006

It is ten o'clock at night and I am sitting uncomfortably on a bus somewhere in New Jersey. The country mother has taken a foray into our nation's metropolis and desperately needs to be planted back in her quiet, contemplative soil.

I hadn't planned on the bus trip this year, but at the last minute I agreed to accompany a group of young people heading to Washington for the March for Life to mark the 33rd anniversary of Roe v. Wade. It is hard to fathom the time that has elapsed since the infamous decision and the impact in lives lost and souls damaged.

I was a senior in high school in 1973 when the headlines hit the papers. As co-editor of my school's newspaper, I penned an editorial that was rife with the righteous indignation of the young. Later as parents, Andy and I explained to our boys in simple terms the issues at stake when a country allows the intentional destruction of the vulnerable and helpless.

When Tim joined our family, the issue became personal. The perfect baby we held in our arms had already won a battle to be born. He had made it safely from the womb to the light of day against the advice and counseling of the voices surrounding his birth mother. We could not imagine his non-being.

Tom likes to think about his little brother's simplicity. He sees it as a wonderful thing. In my mind I view this essential part of his character as a single-hearted, uncomplicated response to life. Tim had a way of cutting to the core of the matter with a child's guileless mind even after his years brought him to the other side of childhood.

In Tim's innocent mind the tiny unborn child was someone to be celebrated and protected. He could see the dark pit swallowing up those adults who could violate their duties of protection and sustenance.

Whoever receives this child in my name receives me,
and whoever receives me receives the one who sent me.
For the one who is least among you is the one who is greatest.

—Luke 9:48

Three years ago Tim rode with me to Washington. He carried a handmade sign that counseled adoption and was decorated with his own baby pictures. He met another young adoptee on the metro and they compared signs and shared smiles.

I felt Tim's presence as I walked today and as we shook our heads in disbelief that big people could be so cruel or clueless. We also felt the pavement shake with the pounding of hundreds and thousands of feet striding along in protest. Tim had thought the bus ride was fun but he'd rather be warm and sitting at home chuckling over his *Umbert the Unborn* cartoon book and praying for all the babies to find good homes. Amen.

Tim had a chance to *be*. That he had that chance, and that our family had the privilege of nurturing that being, gives us cause to praise and thank the Good God, who is Being and in whom we have our own.

> *Truly you have formed my inmost being;*
> *You knit me in my mother's womb.*
> *I give you thanks that I am fearfully, wonderfully made;*
> *Wonderful are your works.*
>
> —Psalm 139:13-14
>
> *Life, especially human life, belongs only to God. For this reason, whoever attacks human life in some way attacks God Himself.*
>
> —Blessed Pope John Paul II, *Evangelium Vitae*

February

February 1, 2006

Though January is history now, we still seem to be stalled in its deep winter slush and cold. Winter in the northeast teaches patience, I think. Just wait and bide your time, be confidently expectant and hope a little, too, and soon the days will lengthen and brighten and warm and become green.

Timothy learned a lot about patience and persistence the year he learned to ski. He was desperately eager to try, and we signed him up at a small ski slope nearby for six weeks of instruction with a group of homeschool students. After the first lesson he was ready to quit. Keeping his balance was difficult and he was afraid of falling. As an experienced parent who had been in this situation before, I reminded him that we had paid for six lessons and he was going to keep coming until the session had ended. All the parents within earshot encouraged him with stories of their first attempts to ski and later success.

In the weeks that followed, Tim started having fun and soon was the one encouraging beginners. Of course, the attention of a patient instructor and some individual lessons helped him along. Two seasons later, Tim and his buddy Justin or his cousins John and Dan or his friends Hannah and Rushton would ride up the lift and ski down until it was time to go home.

Hannah brought all this to mind today. She was to give a speech for the Gavel Club she belongs to and invited us to come and listen. She spoke about death and grieving and gave a friend's remembrances of the fun she had swimming, rock climbing, walking, and skiing with Tim. I listened to her describe Tim breaking off and playing with the huge icicles from the roof of the ski lodge. Hannah then presented me with an icicle she had saved since December and carefully preserved in a little ice chest. It was a tender gesture.

"Omnia in Bonum"

[For those who love God, all things work together for good.]

—Romans 8:28

I lettered this Latin verse in calligraphy and illustrated it years ago to hang on display. After Tim's funeral, I moved the drawing to a wall in the living room where it would catch my eye frequently. I need the daily reminder that God is in

Omnia in Bonum

charge of our universe and our lives and can order even the darkest events for some good. Trusting Him when the good is not yet in focus can be the struggle of a lifetime. Persistence and patience and trust are needed, and I pray for them as my mind sees a gangly Tim swooshing down the hills.

> *Woes? Setbacks deriving from one thing or another?*
> *Can't you see that this is the will of*
> *your Father God who is good and who loves you—*
> *loves you personally—more than all the mothers*
> *in the world can possibly love their children?*

—St. Josemaria Escriva, *The Forge*

February 11, 2006
Our Lady of Lourdes

Today is the World Day of Prayer for the Sick. Andy and I traveled to morning Mass to add our prayers to the voices around the globe petitioning God for mercy for those suffering in body or mind.

My thoughts and prayers focus especially on those with mental illness as I remember Tim's struggles. I must reject the temptation to record only pleasant memories and to edit the past with a blind eye to the difficult episodes that erupted on a regular basis because mental illness was present.

Timothy was a hyperactive preschooler and keeping up with his imaginative mind was a challenge—even for two healthy adults and three older brothers. He would wander off frequently, and his curiosity and impulsivity made for many entries in my notebooks over the years. Our year in West Virginia, when Tim was three, seems to have been the high point in Tim's career of creative mischief, including as it did the following episodes.

At naptime he would routinely empty his bookshelf of books, divest himself of clothes, and climb atop the furniture. He even managed to wander away from our hilltop home and walk down a steep driveway to rearrange mail in a row of rural mailboxes—a federal offense!

One night a wrong number awakened me and I heard laughter coming from downstairs. Investigating, I found Timothy having the time of his life squeezing toothpaste and shampoo all over the floor. I cleaned him up, along with the sticky puddles on the floor, and tucked him back into bed. In the morning when our golden retriever, Ginger, crawled out from under the bed, I discovered that she had been part of his midnight caper. It took me a long while to clean the dried toothpaste and shampoo from her coat.

His fondness for pouring led him to the kitchen where he heaped mounds of powdered soap into the dishwasher and then made sure I knew about it. "Mom, I'm getting into trouble!" On another occasion, his older brother Tom ingeniously devised a siphon from two drinking straws fitted together to suck out the fabric softener that Tim had poured into the lint trap of the dryer. These were just a few of his more printable escapades. We laughed and cleaned up and made more concerted efforts to keep a closer watch on the little imp.

As time progressed we became more concerned. Tim had trouble sleeping, and he hit his head frequently when he became frustrated. He was still a happy inquisitive boy, but he had a difficult time following directions and sitting still. The doctors diagnosed Attention Deficit Hyperactivity Disorder, and then later, when we noticed lots of rapid eye-blinking and throat-clearing, we suspected Tourette Syndrome, which a neurologist eventually confirmed.

This neurological condition, or brain disorder, first exhibits itself as muscle tics that come and go. In Tim's case, the eye-blinking was most commonly followed by jerks of the neck and shoulder. The tics waxed and waned and changed from time to time.

For Tim, the Tourette's also meant other more troublesome conditions: phobias and tendencies toward obsessive and compulsive behavior. He had a fear of moths that prevented him from going through a screen door if any were clinging there, and he would have to sit away from any windows in the house to distance himself from the possibility that a dead moth or fly might be on the windowsill. The other phobia that made all our lives difficult was his fear of the scar on his hand. Tim always kept it covered, either with a long-sleeved shirt or with the ever present band-aid. We learned to make sure there was always an ample supply of band-aids in the house, and I took to carrying a few in my purse.

The compulsive behavior sprang from a need in him to have things "just so." When he played with his small cars they all had to be lined up in rows before he could stop and move on to the next task. The cereal in his bowl had to be poured to a certain level, almost, but not quite, overflowing. When Tim tied his shoes, the leftover laces had to be knotted with as many knots as he could tie. He told himself stories while lying atop his bed and was difficult to budge until he had come to an end. One favorite plot involved finding a doctor who would agree to transplant his brain into the body of a lion.

Life became complicated as the mind demanded things of Tim that neither logic nor persuasion could change. Our search for answers always began and ended with prayer. In between were doctors, tests, medication, therapists, behavior modification attempts, research, and seminars.

We met other parents struggling with the same problems, and other precious children so bright and funny and beautiful and so in need of healing. It kept us anxious at times but always busy bothering God for answers and help.

God hears the cry of the broken-hearted. He helped us cope over the years and He kept Tim under His watchful care. We pray today for our friends who are still struggling and for their children who are still suffering and for all those sick in body or mind. We pray that God may heal our broken-hearted pain, aching for the loss of our dear boy, even while we feel a blessed relief that Tim no longer struggles with the defects he was born with. Through it all, we give thanks to Christ and His Church who are always vigilant and ever attuned to those who are suffering. As St. Teresa of Avila wrote, "With so good a Friend and Captain ever present, Himself the first to suffer, everything can be borne. He helps, He strengthens, He never fails. He is the true Friend" (*The Book of Her Life*, 22, 9).

The crowds still flock for healing to Lourdes where Mary has revealed herself as the compassionate mother. We join them in prayer today and all days:

> *Consolatrix afflictorum*
> *Salus infirmorum,*
> *Auxilium Christianorum*
> *Ora pro eis . . . ora pro me.*
>
> —Litany of the Blessed Virgin Mary

February 14, 2006
St. Valentine's Day

Today is sunny and warm, so unlike our usual February in New England. I took advantage of the break in the weather to venture out to shop for groceries. The store was unusually busy, and then when I noticed the large percentage of people buying flowers and balloons, I realized what day it was. With a gulp, I tried to cover over the empty spot in my heart.

Tim was a great one for showing his love to others. He didn't just wear his heart on his sleeve; it was emblazoned on his chest in superhero fashion. This endeared him to most adults. Who wouldn't feel special when caught up in a hug of mammoth proportions by a beaming child? As Tim grew older and stronger I complained about the pain his hugs engendered and helped him to temper his enthusiasm a bit, but not too much. I dearly miss those strong arms about me and his overt declarations of love and affection. As Tim would say, I'm "hug-deprived!"

Over the years Tim developed a beautiful compulsive ritual, a dialogue that he and I carried out together. It came to precede the bone-crushing hugs:

"Do you love me, Mom?" "I love you, Tim!"
"Will you always love me?" "I'll always love you!"
"Never stop?" "Never stop!"
"Famous words?" "Famous words!"

Now these words are burned into my heart and soul. I love you Tim for all eternity. I wrap my arms around Daddy when I remember your words, and I lay my head upon the Sacred Heart of Jesus who holds us all in His loving embrace.

Life is short. Eternity is forever. Love now!

> *May the Lord make you increase and abound*
> *in love for one another and for all,*
> *just as we have for you, so as to strengthen your*

*hearts, to be blameless in holiness
before our God and Father at the coming of
our Lord Jesus with all his holy ones.*

—1 Thessalonians 3:12-13

*Love can overcome great obstacles,
and God's love can totally transform the world.*

—Blessed Pope John Paul II
Meeting with Charities
San Antonio, Texas, 1987

February 24, 2006

The pounding of the wind against the house woke me early this morning with strong window-rattling gusts of noise. We live on the top of a hill with pasture land around us, so the wind has free rein to rush at us with a galloping speed. It is a pleasant relief in the summer, but it can be brutal in the winter months.

When I heard the wind I remembered how Tim loved to stand outside, arms wide open, and feel the strength of the force pushing him this way and that. He was also fascinated with every weather phenomenon that involved wind, especially hurricanes and tornadoes. I capitalized on this interest of Tim's in our science studies and ordered several books and videos explaining the atmospheric forces at work in these severe cases. He watched the videos so often and with such absorption that he developed a keen weather eye and was always on the lookout for funnel clouds over the back fields. We talked about the mighty power of God who created and put in motion these forces, and Tim was rightly amazed.

Once when he was ten, after he watched a weather video with his sister-in-law, Anya, they had the following conversation:

"So now, Tim, you know how wind is created."

"I don't think so."

She goes on to remind him about high pressure and low pressure systems.

Tim's matter-of-fact reply:

"No, they didn't mention God."

May the simple and childlike hearts forever lead us to consider the self-evident truths that all creation rightly proclaims to those who will hear.

> *Every shower and dew, bless the Lord.*
> *All you winds, bless the Lord.*
> *Fire and heat, bless the Lord.*

FEBRUARY

Cold and chill, bless the Lord.
Dew and rain, bless the Lord.
Frost and chill, bless the Lord.
Ice and snow, bless the Lord.
Nights and days, bless the Lord.
Light and darkness, bless the Lord.
Lightnings and clouds, bless the Lord.

—Daniel 3:64-73

March

March 5, 2006

Winter is still with us here in the hills as bitter cold joins the winds today. Some patches of ground are bare, while the snow piles up in powdery hedgerows where the gusts have driven it. It is sunny this morning, though, and beautiful in its starkness. As I drive down the hill to church this Sunday following Andy, who has gone on ahead in his truck, I am filled with a blessed peace. This bittersweet sensation is becoming a familiar companion, the combination of joy and sorrow that sweeps over me when I remember what our Sunday mornings used to be like.

Tim was never easy to rouse from sleep, but Sunday mornings were always the hardest. He didn't want to leave the comfort and warmth of his bed and, worst of all, put on those "scratchy church clothes" with buttons and zippers and belts. Like all children with sensory defensiveness, Tim couldn't tolerate certain feelings on his skin and his usual uniform was a sweatshirt or cotton t-shirt and "soft pants" as he called them. So we battled each week to get him up and dressed and out the door in time for our little church's only Mass at 8:00 am.

Tim's fertile mind came up with all sorts of reasons he should remain behind. First the usual culprits—too tired and too sick—then as he got older, he reasoned thus: "I'm not Catholic anymore. I think I'll be a Jew, then I won't have to go to church." When I reminded him that Jews believe in God and worship on Saturday, he gave up that idea, but he was still casting about for excuses. I told Tim that he should remember God now so God would remember him when he died. I asked him what he would say to God when he died if he hadn't been to church while he had the chance. Tim thought for a minute and then said, "I'd tell him I was a newcomer!" At that point I tried to hide a smile and continued my insistent prodding to move him along.

Despite all his protestations on Sunday mornings, Tim had that beautifully simple faith that delights parents and without which none of us can enter heaven. He loved to hear stories of the saints and to watch Bible stories on video. One of the last books I read to him was *The Young Faces of Holiness* by Ann Ball, in which she recounts the lives of young people who reached the heights of sanctity. Tim always asked for another chapter and looked long and hard at the photographs.

I picture him this morning communing soul to soul with these same brave little saints as they play before the face of their Father God. It's a comforting image to dwell upon as I put to rest the anxiety of past Sunday mornings and relax in my new-found Sunday peace.

*Have no anxiety at all, but in everything, by prayer
    and petition,
with thanksgiving make your requests known to God.
Then the peace of God that surpasses all understanding
will guard your hearts and minds in Christ Jesus.*

—Philippians 4:6-7

March 10, 2006

A warm wind has blown in over the tops of our hills and melted all but the most stubborn of the snow piles, and no doubt, a few hearts as well. After a brutally cold spell it is a particular joy to watch people's faces as they step out into the 60 degree mildness. There is a thawing of the spirit too.

Today is our grandson Alex's seventh birthday and along with the treasured memories of his babyhood, which I have wrapped in the tissue paper of remembrance and folded carefully away, I remember Tim's joy in Alex, his first nephew. To begin with, it was a matter of titles. It takes a bit of mental gymnastics for a nine-year-old to comprehend the idea of becoming an uncle. All of his uncles were men who hadn't seen their youth in a while. This was beyond his experience.

However, once he laid eyes upon Alexander in the perfection of his infant sweetness, Tim was smitten, and his continual exclamation, "I can't believe I'm an uncle!" was uttered with a smile that couldn't have been broader. He was a frequent adorer of the small baby parts and loved to hold Alex and make him smile. When Alex and his parents moved from Ohio to live with us for a while, Tim was on hand and ever ready for any baby handling short of diaper changing.

When Alex reached his toddler years, he developed into a playmate, and then what fun Uncle Tim could devise! He could make a fort with all the chairs and blankets in the house, quite literally. Ball games and blocks and Lego contraptions and any other entertainment Tim could imagine were brought out for the delight of his nephew. Following Alex came Eddie and then Maxim; at that point there was even more riotous fun in numbers.

When Matthew and Anya moved their family to Mobile in far away Alabama, Tim was devastated and didn't know how he could live without them. His brother Paul and wife

Jasmine solved this problem after a bit when Nicholas, the next nephew, came onto the scene. They lived only a short distance away so Nicholas got to know his Uncle Tim almost as well as his older cousins had.

I am working on a baby quilt now for Nicholas' sister or brother, a niece or nephew who will not have the pleasure of knowing Uncle Tim. As I stitch I feel a momentary

sadness, and then I hear the lisping voice of two-year-old Nicholas, who in his precocious command of the language says, "Tim. Heaven. Happy."

March 28, 2006

Spring has been here officially for over one week now and I am basking in the extra morning light. There is a special quality to the early spring sunshine, and without the leaves to block the sun it streams in through the windows strongly in the mornings. As I look out I see Tim's cat, Apollo, prowling around the yard in search of small prey. Several days ago I watched in amusement as he stalked a flock of turkeys that had ambled into the yard. Apollo maintained a safe distance in an unusual moment of cat savvy, since he was both outnumbered and out-sized.

Tim had a compelling interest in all animals, but the ones that were closest at hand on a daily basis occupied most of his attention and curiosity. Tim and our golden retriever, Ginger, grew up together and shared many an exploit. Ginger would lie peacefully on the floor as Tim lined his little cars on her tawny side. She was equally patient when he sprawled in front of her, mesmerized, as she chewed a rawhide bone to a soft pulp.

Later when a friend gave Tim three ducklings, he would crouch down on his haunches and watch them make their way across the yard in search of forage. Animals seemed to take his presence for granted. The horses on the farm next

door enjoyed a carrot or two when Tim sidled up to the fence and once, a more appreciated repast, when he took the wheelbarrow out to the back field and pulled up the choicest grasses to feed them over the fence.

When he heard of people feeding chickadees by hand, normally rambunctious Tim stood outside in full winter gear and motionlessly waited with cupped hands of birdseed outstretched for the birds he knew would come. His interest in birds continued over the years, and he would perch on top of the kitchen counter, sometimes with binoculars, to watch the birds gliding in to feed at the birdfeeder. Several times he tried to coax a stunned bird back to life after it had flown into our picture window.

The animals most portable and tolerant of his attentions, though, were the cats. We have pictures of Tim holding them as kittens wrapped inside his robe or peeking out from inside his sweatshirt. The creative mind can think of lots of possibilities. One of my favorite photographs shows a smiling Tim standing in front of the barnyard with a tote bag over his shoulder and the white head of the kitten Apollo just visible over the edge.

Naturally, Tim's exuberance and impulsivity often led him to play too roughly with his pets, but a small scratch from a clawed paw can teach a lesson in short order. The lesson Tim taught us was to delight in every creature that

the Good God has placed in our path—to have a sense of wonder and appreciation for the many animals our world abounds in and their myriad and diverse traits.

Apollo has survived the predators for another year. He now just has two middle aged, sedate adults for companionship, but we think of Tim when he jumps upon our laps in the evening, and we remember and treasure our son's joy.

> *Lord, extolled in the heights by angelic powers, You are also praised by all earth's creatures, each in its own way. With all the splendor of heavenly worship, You still delight in such tokens of love as earth can offer. May heaven and earth together acclaim You as King; may the praise that is sung in heaven resound in the heart of every creature on earth.*

—Lauds Psalm-Prayer, Sunday Week III

March 29, 2006
En route to Alabama

Andy and I have left the home place for a journey to Mobile to visit our son and his family. Right now we are soaring over other houses and fields and forests. I still wonder at the whole experience of flying, and I am taken back in memory to Timothy's unforgettable adventure with airplanes.

Mobile was our destination, then, too. Tim's anticipation of flying was like an electric current in its intensity. He couldn't wait, he told everyone he met and had a hard time settling down to any schoolwork in the preceding days. Once we got to the airport in Hartford the excitement mounted, and he made a point of telling the stewardess that it was, "my first time flying." Tim's enthusiasm paid off and he was invited into the cockpit. Of course Andy was ready with the camera.

The moments before take-off were filled with the mantra of his wonder: "I can't believe I'm really going to be flying!" The experience lived up to Tim's expectations, and since it wasn't a direct flight, it was repeated all over again and three more times on the return trip.

I look around today at the seasoned travelers who seem to take this marvel of man's inventiveness and glimpse of the heavens for granted. We glide up above the clouds and no one is hanging onto their window frame and gaping in awe. I think of G.K. Chesterton. "Wonder has the positive element of praise."

I am grateful to Tim for keeping our sense of wonder alive with the forceful power of his childish delight. I think of him now as he enters the realm of heavenly delights before us all.

> *But as it is written:*
> *What eye has not seen, and ear has not heard,*
> *and what has not entered the human heart,*
> *what God has prepared for those who love him.'*

—1 Corinthians 2:9

March 31, 2006
Mobile, Alabama

I sit on the back steps, my hands cupped around an early morning mug of tea, and look out over this yard full of flowering bushes, alive with the sound of southern birds greeting the dawn. The day begins peacefully, and I have a few moments of calm to collect my thoughts before my grandsons bound out of bed to add their chatter to the birdsong. Time with the family is always delightful, but I especially cherish the days spent with Matt and Anya and their boys because distance separates us for so much of the year.

I go back in thought to Tim's babyhood and its impact on Matt's teenage years. Whenever we add to the family circle, it changes the dynamic of family life. For Matt, who was about to turn thirteen and in the middle of a difficult patch of years, Tim's presence laid a balm over frayed nerves and raw emotions. He was a tender big brother and Tim just the happy baby to warm a chilly heart. It did my maternal heart good to see the moody teenager rocking his baby brother, feeding him, teaching him to repeat outlandish phrases, and delighting in his antics. I see the shadow of Matt's love and care for Tim when I watch him with his own sons. It is a double joy.

As Tim got older and Matt went away to school, their time together was limited, but Tim always got a brotherly bear hug and a story at night during the reunions. As I listen to Matthew's nightly ritual with Alex and Eddie and Maxim and hear their anticipation of another "chapter" in their dad's saga of the Canadian superheroes (a washer and dryer named Wally and Dan), I hear an echo of the "Johnny" stories Matt told to a young Tim.

We spent yesterday afternoon touring the Alabama countryside and walking on the beach. At sunset we stopped for dinner at a seafood restaurant. As the hungry children were settled and munching on crackers and Grandpa told stories of his days as a lighthouse keeper, I looked around the table and was struck by the beauty of this family. I thought about the special place each one holds in creating the glory of the whole. All are essential and bring unique gifts that are irreplaceable. As we folded hands to say grace I thanked the Good God for Tim's place in our family and for what his presence had brought to each of our lives. "From thy bounty through Christ, Our Lord. Amen."

April

April 2, 2006

A year ago on this day I was basting the layers of a quilt that was to be a gift for my mother-in-law Mary on her 80th birthday. Friends and family had all signed the pieced squares before they were sewn together, and I was putting in the temporary stitches that would hold everything in place during the quilting process. As I basted, I glanced at the television from time to time to watch the coverage from the Vatican where a gravely ill John Paul II lay near death. About half-way through my sewing I learned that death had come for our beloved Pontiff. Tim came in from his play to watch the images of a world in mourning.

Like so many other loyal Catholic families, our family had a deep, abiding love and respect for John Paul. We read his encyclicals, followed his travels and prayed nightly for him at the conclusion of our family rosary. Tim was excited when we had the chance to attend a papal Mass in Central Park during one of the Pope's visits to America. He watched for a glimpse of the Holy Father and was disappointed that so many people obscured his line of vision.

When Tom traveled to Rome and had his picture taken reaching out to John Paul, Tim was duly impressed. But Tim's love and adulation seemed to peak the Christmas before his death. Tom was studying for the priesthood and had just been sent to Rome the September before. In late December we received a phone call that he had been chosen to serve midnight Mass as an acolyte at St. Peter's Basilica in Rome. Tim couldn't believe it! Watching the Mass on television with the Pope and his brother Tom together, Tim was incredulous. As it so happened, it was the last Christmas on earth for both Tim and John Paul.

I went to a quilt exhibit today in Mobile with my daughter-in-law, Anya, and we admired the expert needlework and design of the quilts on display. As quilters, we both knew the hours of work that went into producing each piece. Often in the middle of the process it doesn't look like much. But, when everything is assembled, the last thread is cut, and you stand back at a distance, the glorious pattern of color and shape comes together to make a work of art. If even a single piece is moved, the design of the whole is changed or ruined.

I think fondly of Tim and the innumerable times he watched me quilting and laying out pieces. Sometimes he helped place the triangles and squares to make the design. I remember the quilts I stitched for Tim, too, and his happiness as he snuggled under them. Mostly, though, I think about the pieces of Tim's life, the circumstances that brought him to us, the people and places that worked together to make the pattern of his earthly days. I can see them a little better now from my vantage point in the middle distance, even as I know with certainty that the full beauty of patches working into design will only be apparent to me in eternity.

Our connectedness to one another, the seams that hold our lives tightly bound as brothers and sisters in the Mystical Body of Christ, join us all firmly in stitches that are invisible and yet eternal. God has the needle in His hand and His inspiration and love for our simple Tim and for His Vicar on earth is the genius that blends these two souls, a world and a life apart, into a glorious whole.

> *The Communion of Saints extends even to the most unfortunate Christian: however much he finds himself on his own, he knows that he never dies alone: the whole Church stands behind him to give him back to the God who created him.*
>
> *The Communion of Saints is a fact that goes beyond time. Each act we perform in charity* [I think here of the prayers Tim said with us for the Pope every evening]

has limitless repercussions. On the Last Day we will be given to understand the incalculable reverberations which the words, actions, or institutions of a saint, and of ours, have had in the history of the world.

—Francis Fernandez, *In Conversation with God*

Each person is a holy moment in history.

—Patrice de La Tour du Pin

April 13, 2006

After our traditional meal of lamb, rosemary buns, and salad with the bitterness of vinegar and herbs, Andy and I drive in the spring warmth to the beautiful Holy Thursday Mass. The evening ride brings us past the river glowing in the western light. Twilight stillness settles over everything and I carry it with me as I mount the steep steps into the hush of the church.

We hear the moving words of this night's ancient liturgy. Words of endless love:

"To share in the supper which Your only Son left to His Church to reveal His love . . . that . . . we might find the fullness of love and life."

"'I give you a new commandment,' says the Lord, 'Love one another as I have loved you.'"

"He loved His own in the world and He loved them to the end."

"I have given you a model to follow, so that as I have done for you, you should also do."

On the way home, with my mind and heart and soul full of love, we pass the cemetery and I think again about Tim's love . . . a recurring theme in my diary of remembrance.

I recall a scene from our year's stay in West Virginia when Tim was about three. He and I were in a tiny grocery store near our rural home, and he was sitting in the grocery cart as I pushed it along the narrow aisles. Shuffling towards us came an unkempt old gentleman with a long beard, rumpled clothes, and a tin can in his shirt pocket to serve as a spittoon for his chaw of tobacco. I mentally shuddered, but Tim was all aglow with bright-eyed interest. The old fellow stopped across from us and looked Tim square in the eyes.

"Hello, little shaver! How are you? Do you want to come home with me?"

Then came the smile that showed a few gray teeth with gaps in between.

Instead of crying or reaching up to Mom for comfort, Tim gave the old gent a beaming smile and said, "Sure!" My

protective instincts urged me to rush Tim out of the store, and only the habit of good manners kept me from bolting.

Over the years I have pondered this scene, and now, in retrospect, with all the intervening years and incidents, I recognize Tim's sweet unguarded love. He saw something lovable and responded, without prejudice or hesitation, to the man from the hills.

Blessed John Paul II expressed Tim's gift beautifully when he said, "How often the shadows of loneliness engulfing a soul can be blown away by the light and warmth of a smile, or of a pleasant word" (Homily, 11 November 1981).

God is love and all love is but a reflection or a response to His first loving us. In order to respond in love to Christ's admonition to love one another, we need to see the image of Christ in all those we meet, especially those who appear to be unlovely or unlovable at first glance. Tim saw Christ's image in everyone he met, not with a conscious vision, but with the instinct of the heart. Living as we do in a world outside the garden, we had to guard him closely because of it. I try to look with new eyes now, though; to blink away the cataracts of prejudice and judgment that make me turn my gaze away from the unwanted and unwashed I see around me.

With Tim's help and example to follow, we can honestly repeat the verse from this night's Mass commemorating love: "The love of Christ has gathered us into one. Let us rejoice and be glad in Him. Let us fear and love the Living God, and love each other from the depths of our heart." And, too, we can echo the response from heart to heart, "Where charity and love are found, there is God."

Another lesson is brought home to us this night from the boy with the big smile and the even bigger heart. In the voice of the cantor Deacon David, another of Tim's friends, we heard these words from Psalm 116:

> *Precious in the eyes of the Lord*
> *Is the death of His faithful one.*
> *I am your servant, the son of your handmaid;*
> *You have loosed my bonds.*

Deo gratias!

April 14, 2006

The procession is always a sober one, no matter what church we find ourselves in for Good Friday. We take our places in line to venerate the cross of our Savior, and as we bend or kneel to kiss the wood, we try to bow our hearts as well so the weight of our own crosses can be borne with love.

This heart-wrenching tradition in the Holy Week liturgy became even more poignant for me the year doctors diagnosed our son Paul with a brain tumor. We learned of it Good Friday morning, and as I approached to venerate the cross in the evening, I laid my mother's tears and fears along with my kiss at the foot of the cross. I tried, as far as I was able, to lay my acceptance of God's will along with them. I think my understanding of Mary's sorrow began that night.

After the heartaches of the past months, I know I have reached a deeper understanding. As I moved slowly up the aisle tonight to add my kiss of love, I joined my own sorrow to our heavenly Mother's as she sat with her dead son and Lord heavy in her arms. Since Tim's death, I have meditated often on this scene. It seems that we can only grasp the trials and tribulations of this earthly life with our eyes on the cross, while at its foot we receive Our Lord's glance of love. And here is Mary, now ours too, to share these trials with us as she lovingly offers the ultimate sacrifice.

In the company of Mary, I have been blessed since Tim's death with the companionship and care of an elite group of women who have surrounded me with their love and prayers: the "club" of other mothers who have each undergone the sorrow of the loss of a child. It is an amazing and beautiful joy amidst grief's dark days—here is the bittersweet again—to be on the receiving end of such love and compassion. I mentally recite the list of their names, both mothers and children, as I give thanks for the Love that prompted them to offer their own to me.

I hear the chant and breathe in the incense as I intone the litany: for Gail and Gregory, for Dale and James, for Priscilla and John, for Karen and Joseph, for Maryanna and Alison, for Ann and Caitlin, for Jenny and tiny Joseph. May our Mother of Sorrows embrace you with her tender love. *Ora pro nobis.*

> *Praised be God, the Father of our Lord Jesus Christ, the Father of mercies, and the God of all consolation! He comforts us in all our afflictions and thus enables us to comfort those who are in trouble, with the same consolation we have received from Him. As we have shared much in the suffering of Christ, so through Christ do we share abundantly in His consolation.*

—2 Corinthians 1:3-5

April 15, 2006

We've come home from the Easter Vigil Mass, and I have tidied the house a bit and spread a clean tablecloth on the dining room table. It's time to sit and have a cup of tea while pondering the great joy of this night's events.

Andy and I both had the same pull on our hearts this evening as we heard the "Alleluias" during the Liturgy. Our first Easter without Tim's fidgety presence next to us and then all of a sudden, with the first Alleluia, he seemed to be there with us, the "Alleluia boy." When he was first discovering language as a toddler, Tim loved to say and sing the word. As he got older we "buried" the Alleluia at the beginning of Lent only to "resurrect" it on Easter.

I go to the china cabinet to find the piece of wood with Alleluia scripted across the front. I set it in a place of prominence in front of the lily and hyacinth and I let the joy push its way to the forefront. Thanks for the reminder, Tim!

> *So you also are now in anguish. But I will see you again, and your hearts will rejoice, and no one will take your joy away from you.*

—John 16:22

April 17, 2006

The joy of the Easter week liturgies spills over and freshens everything visible and invisible. Indoors, the fragrance of the

Easter flowers permeates the air as the sun hits the petals, while outside the spring bulbs are making a gallant attempt to catch up, thrusting their blade-like spears through the soil.

On this day in 2004, Tim was confirmed. Another day of joy. Andy and I had thought for some time that Tim needed the grace of the sacrament of Confirmation, but at fourteen he didn't meet the age requirement at our parish. After we explored several options, he was invited to join the Confirmation class at his Aunt Gail and Uncle Steve's parish in Connecticut, where he could be confirmed with his cousins David and Daniel, who were also fourteen. Tim attended several pre-Confirmation events and a day's retreat given by his uncle, Fr. Jim. We worked together on memorizing the gifts of the Holy Spirit, and I tried to impress upon Tim the effects of the sacrament. He had some anxieties about being singled out in public, but all along we prayed that the Holy Spirit would strengthen him to get through the day.

In a moment of uncharacteristic decisiveness Tim chose his Grandpa Six to act as sponsor, but he agonized when it came time to pick a Confirmation name. We went through the saints books with him and made a long list and then a short list. I had lots of ideas for Tim and tried to steer him in one direction or another. Tim had other ideas, though, and after a week or two he chose St. Zozimus. To begin with, he liked the sound of the name, but after he read a short biography and we did some research together online, a certain suitability emerged.

In Tim's words: "St. Zozimus was born in Syracuse, Sicily, in about the year 570. His parents were rich and owned a lot of land. They dedicated him to St. Lucy and decided when he was seven years old that they would send him to the monastery of St. Lucy near Syracuse. Once, when he was little, he got frustrated because he had to work a lot and he had to be quiet all the time, so he ran away." (I hear a voice from the past. "Mom, let me know if you ever want me to run away.")

Tim goes on to explain that Zozimus eventually became a monk and after 30 years was elected abbot and some years later, bishop.

"He didn't want to be Bishop but he decided that if the people wanted him, he should. He helped the poor and taught his people well. Zozimus lived a good long life and died at the age of 90. His feast day is March 30.

"At first, I liked St. Zozimus for his unusual name, then after I found some information about him, I chose him for my Confirmation saint because he was everything a saint should be. He was a brave bishop and a very holy man. I will try to imitate his bravery."

Tim did imitate his saint's bravery, and with his family praying him on he was able to walk down the aisle toward

Archbishop Mansell. Afterwards he was all smiles and I got the standard huge hug. "I can't believe I just received my Confirmation! I didn't feel the Holy Spirit, though."

We didn't know then that in a little over a year, Tim would depart this world. Looking back, we feel blessed to have followed the inspiration of the Holy Spirit in seeking out the sacrament of Confirmation for our son. Perhaps to some, the last year of his life didn't exhibit a heroic witness to the faith, but we feel certain that this infusion of sanctifying grace helped Tim to acknowledge his Father God at the moment of his death. For this we will be eternally grateful.

> *Recall then that you have received the spiritual seal, the spirit of wisdom and understanding, the spirit of right judgment and courage, the spirit of knowledge and reverence, the spirit of holy fear in God's presence. Guard what you have received. God the Father has marked you with his sign; Christ the Lord has confirmed you and has placed his pledge, the Spirit, in your hearts.*
>
> —St. Ambrose, *De Mysteriis*

> *Indeed the Church desires that none of her children, even the youngest, should depart this world without having been perfected by the Holy Spirit with the gift of Christ's fullness.*
>
> —*Catechism of the Catholic Church*, #1324

April 19, 2006

Two year old Nicholas has spent the night with us. His parents have some pressing business to attend to. It's a lovely day, warm and sunny, but the ground squishes underfoot as Nicholas and I make our way back across the field and turn to walk through the woods. We pass Tim's fort and Nicholas stops to hunt around for treasures. After trudging over roots and fallen trees and skirting the largest boulders, we slowly make our way towards an old stone wall next to the road so Nicholas, whose boyish curiosity so mirrors Uncle Tim's, can watch the roller press down the fresh blacktop. The pure joy of the sun on my head and a small hand clasping mine!

Later the two of us drive to the hospital so Nicholas can meet his new sister, our first granddaughter, Isabella Rose. As we walk towards the hospital I remember so clearly the day Tim and I followed the same path inside to see Nicholas for the first time. Tim held the baby in his arms as well as any uncle four times over and smiled his approval to us.

Life goes on and each new addition is a beautiful blessing from God, a promise to be fulfilled in time and in eternity. I watch Isabella held in her daddy's big hands and offer thanks to God who holds each of us in his palm. May we all express Tim's joy at each new life born into God's plan.

May

May 4, 2006

Spring has come early this year and our usual lengthy "mud season" has failed to make its presence felt with its accustomed mucky grip. The forsythia have bloomed sooner and the trees are blossoming and leafing out. Even taking into consideration the may flies, or black flies as they are more aptly named, it is a joy to be out and working in the garden. I transplanted a tree and worked on rooting out a firmly entrenched bed of bishop's weed.

As I knelt in the garden, I remembered how Tim could sense my moods. If it was a pleasant day and his hug did not help to banish the blues or ease the anxieties, he would give his prescription: "Mom, why don't you go outside and work in the garden?" It was always a sure-fire cure.

I think today of Tim's particularly insightful ability to recognize a need or problem and to want to fix it. When his friend John was in the hospital in Oregon and very ill with leukemia, Tim wanted to help him in some way. His creative remedy was to load a rocket with all the vitamins he could find and send it flying cross-country to John. His suggestion was neither practical nor in the realm of the possible, but that did not deter him from talking to us about the details.

Once during a snowstorm our neighbor Heather came gasping to the door. Her car had slid off the road and in trying to walk home she had an asthma attack. The ambulance had to be preceded by the snowplow, so the wait was painfully long. Instead of panicking Tim had an idea that was both practical and possible. He found and brought Heather the humidifier so she could breathe more comfortably until oxygen arrived. It worked.

My mind makes the connection to the tender compassion God has for each of us. He hears our groaning and has suffered with us through our missteps and our agonies. Tim's compassion reminds us to be always attuned to those who are suffering around us and to offer them our speedy and creative assistance. We look with confidence to our Triune God who in His love has the remedy that will bind all wounds and provide perfect peace.

> *As you did it to the least of*
> *these my brethren, you did it to me.*

—Matthew 25:40

In the tender compassion of our God
The dawn from on high shall break upon us,
To shine on those who dwell in darkness
And the shadow of death,
And to guide our feet into the way of peace.

—Luke 1: 78-79

May 14, 2006

"I baptize you in the name of the Father and of the Son and of the Holy Spirit." We all listened with rapt attention as Fr. Luke pronounced the rite of Baptism and poured water over the baby's head. I corralled several young ones so they wouldn't run freely around the church; family and friends gathered close to the font and Andy was on hand with his camera. We can only fully grasp momentous events upon reflection, though, and when quiet and stillness prevail. I have that moment now as I recall this morning's ceremony.

The sign of the cross is so familiar to us as Catholics that we can easily relegate it to the routine. How many times have we thoughtlessly dipped our fingers into the font with a hasty gesture, and distractedly traced our hand up and down, over and across? Through the words and the tracing and the pouring our new grandchild is brought into the

Family, thanks to the offering of the One on the day the cross became a symbol of salvation instead of infamy.

We stood in Holy Trinity Church, another beautiful and fitting circumstance of the day, and in the name of the Triune God, Isabella was washed clean of the sin of Adam. I hold thoughts of Tim close to me as I remember the many times I climbed those same stairs with him for noon Mass while in town for errands or his classes at the YMCA. I remember his friendship with the Polish priest who was here with us today. I remember his own Baptism, the times when he was little and needed a boost to reach the holy water font, the nights we traced the sign of the cross with our thumbs on his forehead before bed, the mornings before our school day when we blessed ourselves before beginning our studies.

The image that comes next is the day of Tim's funeral when his casket was blessed and brought to the foot of the altar, with the cross his dad made and painted white affixed to the top.

One thing brings to mind another in a rushing wave of memory as I give thanks to God for this day, for our family, for Tim, and especially for our parents whose gift of faith to us makes every joy and every sorrow a Blessed thing.

He predestined us to be His adopted sons through Jesus Christ, such was His will and pleasure, that all might praise the glorious favor He has bestowed on us in His beloved. In Him and through His blood, we have been redeemed, and our sins forgiven, so immeasurably generous is God's favor to us.

—Ephesians 1:4-5

May 24, 2006

In several days there will be over a hundred people here, if my estimates are accurate, and I am all aflutter with list-making and baking and prayers for sunshine.

We have invited family and friends to come to a barn raising. "Calling All Carpenters, Has-Beens and Wanna-Be's" in the words of the invitation. We promised an old-fashioned day with plenty of food, so I am trying to deliver. I miss Tim's hands and young legs in the preparation. I remember how much he loved company of any kind. It was so much easier to commandeer him to help if he knew guests were expected.

Once he'd been released from duty he'd head outside to wait for their arrival. He didn't mind a long wait. Sometimes he'd be on foot or sitting atop the large boulder next to the driveway, or maybe on his bike or even up a tree to get a good look-out. Once he spotted the car, Tim would race inside to give me the good news and then race right back outside again to bombard the passengers with greetings and hugs. Love must be born out in deeds!

I think about the virtue of hospitality and its relation to charity. Love cannot exist in a vacuum; it must be an all-out giving of ourselves, a cheerful and open giving to everyone, not just to those who love us. The word hospitality comes from the Greek and originally meant love of strangers. Tim's big heart wanted to embrace both those he knew and those he didn't with a warm welcome and exuberant display of hospitality. It could be a person walking down the road, our mailman Henry, or a young friend he hadn't seen in five years; he begged to be allowed to invite them in for a tea party. It was a lesson he tried to teach me frequently, but I was too blinded by convention and temperament to learn it well. As we read in the letter to the Hebrews, *Let mutual love continue. Do not neglect hospitality, for through it some have unknowingly entertained angels* (13:1-2).

To make his young friends or cousins or nephews feel at home he would fix a snack of mammoth proportions and outlandish combinations (pickles and brownies come to mind). Tim often concocted a dip out of a strange assortment of condiments from the refrigerator to serve with tortilla chips. When I was working outside, he took particular joy in surprising me with a tray of drinks and snacks, carried out and presented with a happy fanfare. The fact that he was always hungry could have come into play here!

I want to welcome all those coming to help us build the barn with the same joyful expectation that Tim would have shown them. So I mix and bake happily with my nieces who are here early to help put all in readiness, Monica from Virginia and Elizabeth from Pennsylvania. I revel in their young enthusiasm as we cook and clean and carry together.

Later when Andy's cousin Chris arrives from the Boston area, we scrounge around for some cast-off items to make a scarecrow and come up with a yellow rain slicker, mud boots, and garden gloves. We place it at the bottom of our road to point the way to the barn raising. It will stand at attention with one arm raised—and will mightily scare a carload of Tim's cousins as they drive in amidst foggy blackness the night before the big day—but I will have to be the one to offer the happy greeting and the abundant hospitality. I'll have Tim's example in memory, though. Despite his disabilities in other areas, there was nothing handicapped about his heart! I rejoice in the delight of the Lord, who witnessed Tim's gifts of himself, as I put on a smile and follow suit.

God loves the cheerful giver.

—2 Corinthians 9:7

Every person has a basic need to give. The person who does not know how to share with others has a handicapped heart. When we truly give to others, our heart is filled with joy.

—Francis Fernandez, *In Conversation with God*

May 27, 2006

I can't remember ever feeling this tired. I sit with my feet up and a cool drink at hand and try to process the events of the day.

The family had been arriving for days ahead of time and we all scurry in the morning to ready the big screen house for a make-shift chapel. The girls pick flowers for the altar; the nephews hang a crucifix and set out candles, and then bring chairs and rugs for kneeling on the sodden grass. My brother Michael, the choir director, prepares the music and Andy's brother, Father Jim, celebrates Mass for us. We pray for good weather and safety for all those who will be traveling and working alongside us. And we remember the dead . . . Andy's father Joseph, and of course Tim. I think of Tim with joy today. There is much happiness in the air and a sense of anticipation.

Andy has been planning this day for months, and he assembles the carpenters and divides them into teams. After the womenfolk clear up the breakfast debris, I man the camera for a while. People continue to come, the rain holds off, and laughter and the pounding of nails echo across the lawn. What a day to remember! Besides family from near and far, I take pictures of our neighbors, lots of folks from church, and homeschooling friends. There are children everywhere and mothers with dishes in hand and babies on hips. The walls of the barn go up, and then with hands all around and ropes on top, up go the trusses. The men break for lunch and dinner, and we visit and smile over the little ones and compliment the women and ask for recipes. The music comes out, the fiddles and guitars and voices. What joy in hands working together amid love and comradeship. Surely gatherings such as this are a foretaste of heaven.

Some of the boys, Tim's friend Justin and his cousins John and Dan among them, help for a while and then head for the woods. John tells me later that they went to fix up Tim's fort "just the way he always wanted it." They even tack a picture of Tim onto one of the logs.

The carpenters keep working after dinner, and a large group of us gather in the screen house for evening prayer. My heart is full of gratitude for these good people who are praying and working beside me, and as we thank the Father of us all in prayer and song, I feel a powerful longing for that eternal gathering of souls that will praise Him with praise unending.

One thing I ask of the Lord; this I seek:
To dwell in the house of the Lord all the days of my life,
That I may gaze on the loveliness of the Lord
And contemplate His temple.
For He will hide me in His abode in the day of trouble;
He will conceal me in the shelter of His tent.
He will set me high upon a rock.
Even now my head is held high above my enemies on every side.
And I will offer in His tent sacrifices with shouts of gladness
I will sing and chant praise to the Lord.

—Psalm 27:4-6

June

June 7, 2006

One year ago today seemed like a day just like all the other days. It was a Tuesday morning, a warm June day. I prepared Andy's lunch and we chatted as he fixed his morning cinnamon toast and coffee. We discussed plans for our upcoming trip to Alabama. The school year was winding down, and Tim was excited about the vacation just ahead.

Tim and I would go to Mass on Tuesday mornings, so I went in to wake the sleepyhead and try to get him up and motivated to dress in time. Such a normal ordinary day from all outward appearances.

When I opened Tim's door, I still had no clue that anything was wrong. Tim often slept on the floor, sometimes piling all his covers up to make a soft nest. I walked in and saw him lying next to the bed, his head at an odd angle and still my first thought was, "How can he sleep in such an uncomfortable position?" Our minds protect us from the very thought of tragedy. Then I saw his blue pallor and felt his stiff body and screamed for Andy. Tim had taken the soft green tie from his robe and had looped it around the bedpost and around his own neck.

Thankfully, Andy had not left for work yet. He came running at my scream and we cut the tie and laid the poor head of our boy down on the hard wood floor. Andy dialed for help, but I knew no emergency crews would be able to bring the life back into our dear son.

My heart was still protesting even as my mind took in and processed all the facts. "No, dear God, I am not finished with him yet!" I started praying aloud while Andy administered CPR. After the 911 call, the volunteer EMTs began to arrive.

The first on the scene was our friend and fellow homeschooling dad, Pastor Rich Cook, who leads the Congregational Church in town. As more people arrived, he offered to pray with us and I asked him to read from the Psalms. When the police came we were not allowed back into Tim's room, so I paced the floors, praying and trying to calm my racing heart. Compassion was offered to us from the start and I took advantage of all offers, even asking the officers to pray for Tim's soul.

Andy and I shared the task of making the necessary phone calls, first to our own pastor, Father Donald Noiseux (who hadn't yet left the rectory to celebrate morning

Mass), and then the difficult calls to our sons in Alabama, New York, and Massachusetts. I called several close friends nearby and begged for prayers.

Father Noiseux came, bringing with him our deacon, David; he blessed Tim and prayed the prayers for the dead with us. Good manners taught long ago in the heart of the home carried us along, no doubt, but the only real way to explain how anyone can cope with such a situation has to be the grace of God, overflowing and pressed down.

For the rest of the day we were on the receiving end of a heartfelt and steady stream of compassion and love. Our son Paul and daughter-in-law Jasmine arrived, and then our friends Lee and Rich, and Tim and Catherine. Bags of scones and bread and all manner of groceries filled the counters. Our son, Brother Thomas, arrived from the seminary in New York, bringing with him one of the priests of his community. Our friend Dale rushed from her dairy farm in Connecticut with milk and cream and support. My brother Steve and sister-in-law Gail also drove in from Connecticut and were on hand to help us for days. Our son Matthew was making the long drive from Alabama, and my parents were heading back from a trip visiting family in Illinois.

Everyone who came knew Tim well, his enthusiasms and his difficulties. All consoled us with the fact that he could not have made a conscious decision with the full consent of his will. Obsessive thoughts and the compulsion to carry them out seemed to have claimed our son's life in the end. While this thought was comforting to us as far as his eternal salvation was concerned, the bold face of loss and grief seemed ever present. Perhaps the newness of the loss and the prayers begun for Tim and for us that morning, coupled with the grace of the present moment, were what worked together to see us calmly through the day.

There were many consolations. Tom's fellow Legionary, Father Todd, said Mass for our family group that afternoon at our little parish church, and afterwards he and Brother Thomas sang a beautiful litany of the saints. Dale went home to Connecticut and in prayer was led to a marvelously personal Bible verse:

> *My brothers, I beg you to bear with*
> *this word of encouragement,*
> *for I have written you rather briefly.*
> *I must let you know that your*
> *brother Timothy has been set free.*

—Hebrews 13:22-23

The circle of love surrounded and held us. With everyone doing his part in the great plan of God, we made it through the first day and woke up the next morning to console each other and make plans for the wake and funeral.

A year has gone by since Timothy's death. At Mass this morning I offered my thanksgiving to the Good God, Lord of the living and the dead, for Tim's life and for the many dear ones who made his death bearable and speeded his entrance into the heavenly realm with their prayers, Masses, alms, and acts of charity.

> *In the morning You fill us with Your love;*
> *We shall exult and rejoice all our days.*
> *Give us joy to balance our affliction*
> *For the years when we knew misfortune.*
>
> —Psalm 90

June 11, 2006

Looking back, I find it hard to imagine how we coped those first few days after Tim's death. I know for certain we were carried forward on a great tide of grace. It pushed us along to accomplish the necessary tasks when Andy and I were incapable of coherent reasoning.

We traveled down the hill to arrange for the funeral and to choose a burial plot, decisions that must be made quickly. Condolences poured in.

The visible compassion took many forms, from a neighborly knock on the door with gifts of food, to telephone calls and cards from those far away. Envelopes containing money were handed over with a hug and helped us pay all the expenses that an unexpected death demands. A collection from Andy's co-workers at the college, his mother's emergency fund, a hefty check from the youth group at our parish, a sacrificial gift from a beloved aunt, and countless other envelopes large and small mounted up; compassionate gestures that enabled us to bury Tim with dignity.

Andy was determined to build Tim's coffin. This desire was born from a discussion we had years before. We each preferred the simplicity of a plain wooden casket. Shortly after our talk I happened to discover a set of plans to build one. I filed them away and forgot them. Now was the time to bring them out.

What a blessing it was for Andy, for our sons, and for my father to have their hands busy on that task. They bought some ash and maple boards, friends came by with tools to lend, and the barn became a workshop humming with the sounds of sawing and hammering.

I remembered the quilt I had made for Tim's bed; it had been folded in the mending basket for years. I had made it of large and small rectangles, and squares of red and blue and brown. Quilted in the center of the large squares were

JUNE

crosses and anchors and hearts, symbols for faith, hope, and charity. Little did I know when I assembled the patches, quilted it with my mother, and watched Tim drive his toy cars over the rectangular "roads," that it would be his burial quilt one day.

We laughed and cried over the photographs that Matthew assembled into a collage for the wake, and I pulled out Tim's portfolio of school assignments and pictures to bring along. Tom and Andy and I wrote an obituary, trying our best to find the words that would give honor to Tim's short life. Friends and garden club members dropped off buckets of garden flowers so we could arrange some simple baskets to grace the funeral home, the church, and the cemetery. More friends stepped forward to lend us a trailer and offer us their homes for family coming in from out of town.

In the midst of the crush of grief, we felt a great joy at the generous gifts poured out for us. The greatest gifts were for Tim because prayers were what he needed most, and what we craved for him. The Masses said, the rosaries, and the prayers of the children touched our hearts.

When we assembled for the wake and saw the lines of people that stretched out into the halls of the funeral parlor, we felt another surge of joy. Tim came from a little town, and he was not well known in any of the ways that teenagers come to be known—through sports or academic achievements or volunteer work. Yet here were all these people, some who only knew Tim by his smile and exuberant hello, come to say good-bye, to offer a prayer for him, and to give us their sympathy. There were big guys that shed manly tears over Tim's death, friends from long ago who traveled hours to be with us, family who anticipated every need, lots of Tim's young friends who cheered us with their sweet selves, and college friends who touched us with their inspired compassion. I wore one such show of tender compassion on a ribbon around my neck. Our dear friends Priscilla and Roger, themselves veterans of grief, loaned us a relic of St. Faustina which arrived from Florida by overnight mail.

We laughed over the mistake that left behind a large basket of flowers I had arranged, the "premier" arrangement, and brought in its place a plastic paint bucket of left over rhododendrons. Tim would have laughed at that, too. Again joy poured and swirled around with the sorrow. We felt God's hand of comfort atop our bowed heads. We held tightly to our faith that the love and care which had brought Tim into being and had followed him through all the happy and difficult years was even now helping us to honor the left-behind temple of his body, even now, as the angels carried his soul to that spot with God reserved for Tim since the beginning of time.

The day of the funeral was hot and sunny. We traveled down the mountain again to the funeral home in Westfield with our cortege of cars. After prayers led by Uncle Father Jim, Andy gave Tim his last haircut, and this time the locks were not swept up, but carefully preserved as relics. We said our last farewells, and with the incongruous sound of a cordless screwdriver Andy secured the top of the casket, the white wooden cross now visible.

Back in our cars we drove in the brilliant sunshine beside the river, past our tiny parish church which was too small to hold all of us, and over the green bridge to St. Thomas church. Inside, Andy and I "dressed" Tim one last time as we unfolded the burial pall and spread it over the simple coffin of our boy. The funeral Mass spread the balm of Divine Love over the fresh wound. Those of us who had known and loved Tim, and a good number who were just now beginning to know and love him, shared in the Mass' gifts of music and song and Word and grace. Afterwards, the pallbearers—his brothers Matt, Tom, and Paul; Grandpa Six; his Godfather, Uncle Dan; and Tim's tall friend Justin—grasped the brass handles and carried Tim out into the sun, and a few minutes later to his graveside between the river and the hills.

With his cousins and Aunt Julia and Uncle Mike providing the harmonious backdrop in song, we prayed again, and then left the shell that was once Timothy Andrew Zozimus Montanaro behind.

The parade of cars followed us back up the hill to home for a grand picnic with laughter and only a few tears in evidence. Tim's climbing tree was full of cousins, and

JUNE

a grandpa too. Friends spilled out from the house and onto the porch and into the barn and over the fields as we ate, played, and remembered Tim. Zoë and her dad, Phil, brought out their fiddle and guitar and offered their gifts of music as we feasted on the food, tables groaning under the weight of it all.

It was a fine day and a fitting end of the chapter marked "This Life."

> *May flights of angels lead you on your way*
> *To paradise and heaven's eternal day*
> *And bid you enter Sion's light!*
> *May choirs of angels sing you to your rest*
> *With once poor Lazarus, now forever blest!*

—Requiem Mass, "In Paradisum"

June 13, 2006

June 13 is the feast of St. Anthony, who is so often depicted with the infant Jesus in his arms. It is also the anniversary of Tim's First Communion day.

Due to Tim's distractible and excitable nature we had requested that he receive his First Communion at a Saturday morning Mass with just family and his church friends present. We hoped that a quiet setting might help Tim feel more inwardly composed and aware of the day's significance.

At home we helped him dress in his white shirt, tie, and navy blue pants, and then we drove down the hills to our little brown church in the valley. There we had the privilege of bringing our son to the steps of the altar where Jesus was waiting for him.

We found that preparing our children to receive the Eucharist was a great blessing and an awesome responsibility. To see an eager child, empty of the marks and scuffs of serious sin, respond to the eternal invitation of Love has been one of our most sublime joys. When God added to our family the simplicity and insights of a mentally challenged child, our joy reached a completely new level. We used a miniature Mass kit with small vessels and cloths, read the stories of young Eucharistic saints, and prayed that God would supply our deficiencies with an increase of grace.

Tim bounced and glided happily through the Mass and received Our Lord with due solemnity when the time came. He posed for pictures afterwards and was most gleeful about the refreshments downstairs in the hall. One of his church friends, a grandfather as well as the parent of his own special child, presented Tim with a box of three small ducklings. Now Tim's joy was boundless.

One of the first masses offered for Tim's soul after the funeral had been on June 13th at another small church in West Warren, about an hour away from home. As I drove to that Mass by myself in the early morning, I had plenty of time to meditate on the gift of Love in the Eucharist, Body, Blood, Soul and Divinity, that Tim had received and whose presence had filled him with "every grace and blessing."

How fitting for this Mass to be said on the anniversary of his First Communion.

We are not often aware of the workings of grace in our souls, but we trust that God supplies all that is needful. On the rare occasions when we are blessed to see what God has accomplished we need to respond with our thanksgiving of love.

My thanksgiving a year ago as I drove back to the home hills was for many dear people. It was for my friend Karen, herself a member of the club of sorrowing mothers and also mother of her own challenged child, whose alms had arranged for the day's Mass; for Fr. Becker, the celebrant, whose generosity and radiant presence had long been a gift to the families in our homeschooling group; for the Franciscan nuns present, whose words of love and compassion were like balm on this mother's heart. And of course, it was mostly for my own Tim, so newly lost and so greatly loved.

On top of everything was the great Thanksgiving to our God, the giver of every good gift, who had brought us all together in His Love that morning.

> *Jesus, Lord and God of all*
> *Come to us we pray*
> *Thus united in your love*
> *May we live this day.*

June 19, 2006

Today is another day of remembrance: our 30th wedding anniversary. My parents join Andy and me for a Mass of thanksgiving, and then we head to a restaurant in the country for breakfast. We have tried, over the years, to spend a day or several days together on the occasion of our anniversary. Spending time alone with each other creates a nice pause in the hectic pace of work and family life and child rearing. We can catch up and reconnect in order to keep the bonds of love entwined and unfrayed.

Andy has a hard time this year walking away from the unfinished barn to spend that time apart, but it will be good for him to step back from the urgent call of hammer and nail, level and saw. And good for me, too, to spend some time with him alone, without the barn looking over his shoulder.

On the drive to Lenox we both remembered Tim's funny expression whenever he'd see us embracing. "Ah, romance!" I'm not sure where he picked it up—maybe from the scene in *Lady and the Tramp* where the title character dogs are sharing a plate of spaghetti to the tune of Italian accordion music. Someday, I'll have to watch it with the grandchildren and find out.

Tim grew up knowing that visible expressions of love were important, and he took them for granted. When he was 10, I recorded this comment, delivered to Andy after he arrived home from work: "Hurry up and change, Dad. Get a snack and have a little romance so you can come out and play." "Romance" for Tim meant "Kiss and hug Mom."

Tim often needed us to express our love for him in a tangible way, too. If we were not quick enough to take the hint, he'd tell us he was "hug-deprived." The group hug or huggle was a favorite adaptation for Tim.

He also disliked discord in the family and was eager to promote reconciliation and peace if he was within earshot of an argument. The hug was his cure-all remedy and prescription.

This year our anniversary trip to Lenox was particularly quiet. We went midweek and in the off season, so we had the historic inn to ourselves and breakfasted alone in the dining room the next morning. We found a beautiful old stone church for morning Mass, and there we thanked God for the gift of our marriage and for the children and grandchildren He had blessed us with. We also gave thanks for the graces of the sacrament of marriage that had helped us weather the storms and squalls along the way. Our love, Tim's love, God's love. Love unending!

"Ah, romance!"

> *To fall in love with God is the greatest of all romance;*
> *To seek Him, the greatest adventure;*
> *To find Him, the greatest human achievement.*
>
> —St. Augustine

June 21, 2006

It was late afternoon as I backed out of Joan's driveway to begin the hour's drive back home, the car laden with sewing machine, ironing board, and quilts. I had spent the day with a group of mothers and daughters of varying ages for an event Joan billed as "Lost Arts Day." We had chatted and feasted on lovingly prepared food and had taught some of the needle arts to the uninitiated. It was a day filled with laughter and joy, elements provided in large part by Joan's brood of happy children. After mentally replaying the past hours, my thoughts turned to laughter and joy in themselves and then, following a natural progression, to Tim.

Children always bring joy into a house and much occasion for laughter, but when Tim became part of our family there was an exponential increase in the joy factor. His laughter was contagious, and his antics elicited our laughter as well. Even the mischief that had to be reprimanded had us laughing out loud or behind a hand.

Tim's experiments with food coloring and lipstick come immediately to mind. Then there was the period when he pretended to be a dog and drank from puddles in the driveway and wagged his "tail" at church. As he got older he watched vintage cartoon videos, Heckel & Jekyll and Wally

Gator mostly, and their particular brand of slapstick humor had him laughing hysterically. Later he discovered Laurel and Hardy with the same effect.

One day I heard Tim laughing uncontrollably and went in search of him to see what was so funny. He was "reading" the *Where's Waldo* book and was stuck on the clown page: pies flying, flowers squirting and hundreds of other tiny images. His imagination was supplying all the details as he pored over the pictures.

Our joy was sometimes simply witnessing Tim's very large capacity for joy and his ready laughter. Often it was a glimpse into the workings of his mind that brought our chuckles, for he had a very literal understanding of the conversations around him. At the dinner table one night we heard Paul explaining about the prototype of an electric airplane that the designers hoped would catch on as a commuter vehicle. Tim listened silently for a long while and then commented, "Well, I guess you'd need an awfully long cord!"

As I near home I thank God for the years of Tim's joy and laughter that cheered our souls. I give thanks for the joys of childhood that we too often forget in the headlong rush for comforts and wealth. I am glad that Andy and I did not weigh the question of another child against the bottom line of expenses and lost leisure.

As I pull into the driveway, I remember suddenly: soon the house will ring with young voices, for Matthew and the Alabama boys will be arriving tonight. Time to get ready for the joy!

June 23, 2006
Feast of the Sacred Heart

Our family has a long history of devotion to the Sacred Heart of Jesus. Even before we were married, Andy's family in New York and mine in Missouri placed images of the Sacred Heart prominently on the wall. It was only natural, then, that this love learned in the heart of our two families be preserved and expressed when we married and our own children were born. We had the Enthronement of the Sacred Heart in our home and came to depend on the promises of Jesus given to St. Margaret Mary Alacoque to those who honor His Sacred Heart. Of the twelve promises, we came to focus particularly on this one: "I will establish peace in their own families."

When Tim was a baby and the bickering and fighting of his older brothers threatened the joy of family life, Andy added a little addendum to our meal prayers: "Sacred Heart of Jesus, bring peace to our family." It was short, and one of the first prayers Tim could say. He was proud to be able to add his voice to those about the table.

As he got older, Tim seemed especially sensitive to those around him who were not at peace. He brought his hugs and sometimes his advice. (Who would have known that he was absorbing what we told him when he was the one in the throes of an argument!)

But, as Ronald Knox says so aptly in one of his sermons, "Peace, in the Christian sense, is a threefold gift, and the world only offers one third of it. True peace means peace with God, peace within ourselves, and peace with one another."

As parents we were eager not only for our sons to act peaceably towards one another, but also for them to make peace with God. For Catholics, this means going to confession. Confession was always a challenge for Tim. I tried to help him examine his conscience, made sure he actually entered the confessional, and had to remind him to say the penance he was given by the priest.

Together with our Catholic homeschooling friends we gathered on the First Friday of each month to honor and make reparation to Jesus in his Sacred Heart. Confession was part of the day.

On the first Friday in June, just days before his death, Tim and I arrived at St. Thomas for our monthly homeschooling

Mass. As we knelt before the Blessed Sacrament, I told Tim it was his turn to go to confession. He was in one of his resistant phases, mental illness and original sin working together to make life difficult for himself and for others. He replied, "I'm not the kind of person that can tell myself what to do." I looked at Our Lord in the monstrance and begged His help. How should I respond to that kind of convoluted thinking?

Several minutes later, I turned to him and said, "Tim, go to confession." As he immediately got up and left to find Father in the confessional, I whispered my heartfelt prayers of thanksgiving that I had been given the right words. As it happened that was the last confession on earth for Tim.

Today I hold in my hand a relic of St. Margaret Mary Alacoque, another loan from Priscilla and Roger, and I pray to this little apostle of the Sacred Heart for true peace for our restless hearts. I beg the loving heart of Our Lord that the peace Tim now experiences will be the peace our family continues to strive for as we beg at every meal and in union with all who sit at our table, "Sacred Heart of Jesus, bring peace to our families."

> *Agree with one another, live in peace, and the God of love and peace will be with you.*
>
> —2 Corinthians 13:11

JUNE

Today we pray to the Mother of the Eternal Word so that the Heart of Jesus, the "furnace burning with charity," may never cease to burn within the horizon of the life of each one of us. We pray that He may reveal to us the Love that is never extinguished or diminished, the Love that is eternal. We ask that His love may give light to the darkness of our earthly night and give warmth to the cold hearts of men.

—Blessed John Paul II
Angelus, 23 June 1985

July

July 1, 2006

It was a perfect summer day, just right for a drive and an outing. Matthew and I loaded his boys into our two cars, and we headed south armed with snacks and drinks and Tim's walkie-talkies. These last were our gift to Tim one Christmas, in the hope that they would keep me from worrying when he went off on a hike or a bike ride down the country roads. Now they are a low-tech alternative to a cell phone, and they help keep our two vehicles in contact as we navigate the highways.

After several hours we pick up Brother Thomas at the seminary and drive a bit further to an old art-deco amusement park on Long Island Sound. No matter what we choose to do, our visits with Brother Thomas are days of happiness. At best we can see him once a month, and if he is out of the country we can only stay connected by phone or email. Today we were happy again to be together: on the Ferris wheel, in the paddle boats on the lagoon, and later in the shade on the grounds of the Center for Higher Studies where Brother Thomas' pastoral ministry and formation continues these days.

Tim was in the background of my thoughts, especially images of the trips Tim and Andy and I enjoyed with Tom in the months before Tim's death. Tom is quick to point out God's hand in the arrangement of it all. He had been studying in Rome and expected to be there for another year or two. When he was given a different assignment in New York just six months into his Italian sojourn, Tom wondered what surprises God had in store for him. As it happened in God's providential design, he was able to spend some time in Tim's company in the spring months and was only several hours away on the day of his death.

The last visit the four of us had together was particularly memorable. We spent a glorious day at a state park and hiked, played baseball, watched turtles in a pond, and shared a grassy meadow with a family of deer. Andy kept the camera busy and now we can look at the pictures and remember: Tom and Tim running through the waist high grass, climbing the boulder near the picnic site, and relaxing together after lunch. God is good.

As we caravanned back home to the hills this evening, with sleepy boys sprawled about, I had ample time to reflect and praise God for all His plans, those so evidently for our

good and those which will remain a mysterious puzzle until the light of God's eternal love shines upon them. For each and every one I give thanks, now and forever.

> *Insofar as we know ourselves to be children of God,*
> *Life becomes a continual act of thanksgiving.*
>
> —Francis Fernandez, *In Conversation with God*

July 16, 2006

Today we've traveled to the big woods, that part of upstate New York that borders the Adirondack Park and where my parents live in a log cabin on twenty acres of rock and trees and hills and lake. They've named it "Hearthstone," the inspiration being an old sampler that was a wedding gift to my grandparents.

> *Burn fire, flicker, flicker flame.*
> *Whoso shall stand on this hearthstone*
> *Shall never, never stand alone.*
> *Whose hearth is cold,*
> *This hearth is his home.*

It's a lovely sentiment and one which fits my parents well. Their charity extends far beyond the family circle.

Tim loved his grandparents dearly—or maybe fiercely is a better word, as they were often the recipients of his strong-armed hugs. Tim became my father's shadow over the years, as well as his helper and playmate, since Grandpa has always worked hard and plays just as hard. His patience with Tim, who had the ability to try anyone's reserve, was admirable.

Tim hammered, lugged wood, and handed Grandpa his tools. When it was time for a break, Tim learned the finer points of chess and poker, scrabble, puzzles, and golf. Grandpa is not content with mediocrity, so teaching is always a big part of the play. Tim grew to love it all, but especially the golf lessons; here his natural talent helped him along. He remarked to me once that "Grandpa may not be a professional golfer, but he's the best golf teacher there is!" Part of the fun of learning golf at Hearthstone had something to do with the floating golf balls whose target was the lake. Later, with a large net, the two of them would set out for a paddle in the canoe to retrieve the balls. What fun!

Of course, Grandma was always busy in the kitchen and had all the favorite foods ready. Besides that, she was ever at hand to read a story or share in an adventure, was a partner in most of the games, and the organizer of "Bingo with Prizes." It's not hard to see why Tim didn't ever want to go home when the visit was over.

Today Tim's nephews, Alex and Eddie and Maxim and Nicholas, will enjoy the attention of their Great Grandpa. They will put up tents and then grab the canoe paddles as we all head down the bumpy road to the lake in his rusty old truck. Great Grandma has the picnic lunch ready.

I am reminded of Alex's musing from several years' back. "Grandparents are a gift from God." (His words were misinterpreted by his dad at first, who heard, "Green pants are a gift from God." Uproarious laughter followed the translation!)

Yes, indeed, they are a gift, and when they pray just as hard as they work and play, the gift is that much more valuable. To those of us who have been blessed to grow up in the arms of loving families, the image of God as Father is so familiar and natural. Tim had the benefit of both a loving father and two beloved grandfathers. Now his soul rests within the embrace of the ultimate Father. How grand.

Behold what manner of love the Father has bestowed upon us, that we should be called children of God, and such we are.

—1 John 3:1

July 18, 2006

Wandering outside in the early morning stillness, I walk around the partly finished barn. The walls are up and the green metal roof panels are halfway across the span of trusses. It is still hard to believe what has been accomplished on this spot since this day last year when the charred timbers of what had been a barn greeted my return home from a trip into town.

Just six short weeks after Tim's death, a second disaster occurred that could easily have been a tragedy. I had left a quietly napping house to go down the mountain for groceries. Matthew was sleeping with Alex and Maxim, and I had just read Eddie his books and covered him with a quilt, thinking him to be sound asleep.

On my way home several hours later, my thoughts ran to putting the food away and surprising the boys with the pizza I had in the car. These thoughts fled when I saw the fire and rescue trucks at the base of our hill and the hoses snaking up from the hydrant there. Now in a panic, I drove up the hill and found a mother's second worst fear . . . *fire*!

In our small town with a volunteer fire department, many of the firemen are our neighbors. One of them, Kate, allayed my gravest fear—no one was hurt. With heart thumping, I surveyed the scene: the smoking blackened shell of our barn, three or four fire companies sitting and resting with water bottles, white foam everywhere. Then I saw what I was so anxiously searching for, the faces of Matthew and my grandsons. Praise the Good God.

Piecing together the story after the culprit's confession, we found out that Eddie had gotten up while everyone else slept. The curious five-year-old had headed for the barn where the three chickens we'd been given several days before were settling into their new coop. After playing with them for a while, he spied some matches from the previous night's grilling and somehow managed to reach them.

Boys and matches seem to have a magnetic attraction. My own grandfather tells the story of how he and his brother, sneaking a smoke in the hayloft, burned down the family barn in Illinois. Tim had his own fascination with matches and fire, but nothing as serious as this resulted.

Eddie's adept fine motor skills soon mastered the art of striking matches, and fire broke out in the chicken coop where dried hay was spread all over the floor. The coop opened out into the main part of the barn but also had a smaller chicken-sized door which exited into the fenced barnyard. Eddie saw the smoke-filled barn and wisely opted to go out the chicken door. He and the chickens crawled out and he ran, scaled the chain link fence, and then woke up his dad and told him to call 911.

I have no doubt that my grandson's guardian angel was at work aiding his escape from the burning barn, but I also have a strong intuition that Tim's intercession from heaven played a part in making sure we had no more unexpected deaths that summer. Tim had always been vigilant with his nephews' safety and had saved a boy or two from harm on several occasions. The fact that the chicken door had no handle on the inside and opened from the outside in, leaves an even stronger impression that miraculous aid was given. We were also blessed with the direction the wind was blowing on that very hot day. If it had been otherwise, we would have lost the house as well, instead of losing just one of its windows cracked from the heat of the fire.

After the ordeal was over, I sat with the children on a blanket in the front yard and we ate the pizza I'd brought for them. My gaze rested on each dear face as I thanked God, the angels, and Tim for their safety.

The saints intercede for men. The guardian angels not only pray for men, but they carry out duties towards them. If intercession takes place through the blessed in Heaven, through the guardian angels there is both intercession and divine intervention; they are at the same time advocates for men before God and ministers of God before men.

—G. Huber, *My Angel Will Go Before You*

For He will give His angels charge of you
to guard you in all your ways.
On their hands they will bear you up,
lest you dash your foot against a stone.

—Psalm 90: 11-12

July 21, 2006

I help Matthew load the last of the luggage into the car, make sure Alex and Eddie and Maxim are well buckled up in the back seat, and pass out bags of small toys and games to keep them occupied on the long drive from Massachusetts to Alabama. The car crunches over the gravel as it leaves the driveway, and I hear the boys' last farewell cries, "Good-bye Grandma, I love you!" Then they are lost to view as the car disappears down the hill.

Another day of farewells accompanied by a sense of melancholy emptiness. I have a hard time making the transition from a busy Grandma whose days are filled with feeding and entertaining these lively boys to the solitary wife going about her days in quiet.

As I strip the sheets from the beds, put away the toys, and wash the breakfast dishes, I call to mind Tim's even greater difficulty with good-byes. For someone whose whole being entered into the present, whatever that occupation or event happened to be, transitions were always hard. Factor in Tim's exuberant joy at being with family and friends and a child's sometimes dismal view of school, chores, and bedtime, and you get a pretty good idea of the challenges we faced when confronted with leave-taking. By far the biggest hurdle was getting Tim to accept the inevitable: "It's time to go." Once this was accomplished, he could often be persuaded to enter wholly into the act of bidding farewell. The strong hugs, a promise to come back soon—or if we were at home, the quick dash to his room to present the parting favorite with some treasure from his collection of rocks or cars or toys.

Somehow I always see an image of the Ascension when I am pondering difficult good-byes. Yes, Our Lord ascended gloriously, but He also left behind a mother who would miss His material presence to a degree commensurate with her ability to love, and a band of followers who must now exist without Him and His physical proximity. It surely was a difficult transition. But Mary, the apostles, and the other disciples responded as Jesus had instructed, with concerted prayer for the coming of the Holy Spirit.

And that is how I have peacefully weathered Tim's big good-bye and how I will continue to bear it until we see each other again in the bright light of God's love.

I hear a little voice from days past:

"Mom, what is Jesus' last name? I think it must be 'Heaven.' We're going to see the Heavens!"

We live in hope.

July 25, 2006

It is mid-morning on one of those near-perfect summer days in the hill country . . . a few fair weather clouds in a pale blue sky, with a breeze that neither chills nor scorches. The perfect day to hang out laundry on the clothesline. Ours is stretched between Tim's favorite climbing tree and a large white pine. As I clip the clothes to the rope I think of a conversation I had with several friends after Mass on Sunday.

Carol was reminiscing about her mother Eva, who died some months ago. Eva was from the old school where any cleaning was concerned, but she had a particular affinity for the cleaning of laundry. She took meticulous care of her clothes and linen and loved to bring things out to the clothesline to dry. There was a system to it, though; no slapdash hanging for her. Carol said one of her mother's highest compliments was, "You put out a beautiful wash!"—an accolade which Carol herself earned before her mother's death.

I think of that and chuckle as I hang out the wash on the line. I remember Tim's attempts at helping with this job and shudder to think what Eva would have said had she seen his efforts.

I regularly had Tim help with the laundry, and as he got older he was supposed to do his own wash: hauling the clothes to the basement, sorting and washing, and then drying the clothes on the line or in the dryer. Tim often balked at the idea of using the clothesline since the dryer was so much easier, but after he started pinning up the clothes, he would warm to the task, or rather, his fertile imagination found a way to make a game of it. Clothes would be pinned any which way or stretched across both lines in tent fashion. One day after setting him to the task of hanging a blanket on the clothesline, I looked out to check his progress. I wondered what was taking him so long and could only laugh when I discovered the reason. Tim had taken every single clothespin out of the bag to use in hanging the blanket. No wind could whip this one from the clothesline!

Taking clothes down was a different story. He seemed to delight in yanking the clothes off the line without first unpinning them. Perhaps it was a game to see how far he could make the clothespins fly. In any event, we ended up with more clothespins on the ground than in the bag.

Tim and Eva shared a sweet repartee as the years went by, meeting up when we visited with Tim's church friends. Over coffee and doughnuts after Mass on Sunday mornings the two would tease and laugh, Tim always finishing up with a smiling admonition to Eva: "Be good, now!"

Eva had been diagnosed with Lou Gehrig's disease and was too sick to attend Tim's funeral, but I knew she'd be praying. We often sat behind her in church and had glimpsed the well-worn prayer book held together with rubber bands. When I saw her for the first time after the funeral, she was being pushed down the aisle in her wheelchair. Her lingering

JULY

glance held a loving compassion, the kind only a fellow-sufferer can give. No words were needed when the eyes spoke so clearly.

Every day seems to bring with it a score of memories, and I hang them out on the clothesline of my heart and watch them flap in the breeze. Tim and Eva are both finished with laundry now and with sorrow, but I still take delight in the hanging as I think and pray and smile.

When young people like you or older people like me take the time to meet one another and to show their friendship, simply and sincerely, to help one another as best they can, that is happiness on earth!

—Blessed Pope John Paul II
Speech to Youth, Montreal 1984

August

August 5, 2006

The heat wave of the past week is over now and it is cool and pleasant in the early hours of the day. The crows are raising a ruckus outside and provide a sharp contrast to the peace and quiet within. The house has been full of guests all week and my hands have been busy with many tasks. As a result, the weeds have taken over in the gardens. I go out and try to bring some order to the chaos. I love being on my knees in front of a flower bed. The colors and shapes of the flowers and leaves grab my attention and, already in the attitude of prayer and reflection, I can give time to both as my hands keep busy with the weeds and spent blossoms.

I remember Tim spending time in the garden too. We started seeds inside and later planted the small seedlings when the weather warmed. Tim was fascinated with the whole process. He liked to check to see if anything had sprouted and then to watch the progress as the minute plants put out leaves. In typical boy-fashion, digging in the dirt was popular but weeding was not. Harvesting was definitely the most fun, and the enjoyment was multiplied if you liked the taste of what you were picking.

Take the raspberries, for instance. Tim had a knack for finding ripe berries, and he would gravitate towards the raspberry patch when he first went outside. He initiated his friends and cousins and nephews into the art—or perhaps the stealth—of raspberry picking; no equipment needed if everything you pick goes immediately into your mouth.

We planted bird house gourds one year, and Tim watched as the vines quickly covered the rustic trellis we had built. These gourds are not edible, so our harvesting resulted in large mounds of pale green gourds with long straight or curved necks. I took a picture of Tim surrounded by the piles of them.

Several years the peach crop from our single tree was large enough to fill buckets and baskets worth of fruit. As Tim delighted in abundance of any kind, seeing all the peaches together gave him joy. Green beans and cherry tomatoes, on the other hand, were small enough to disappear directly into the mouth like the raspberries, and he experimented with feeding them to the dog, too.

There are so many images in the Bible that are familiar to the farmer or gardener. But the world is so full of growing things that, gardener or not, we can readily relate to the lessons being taught. The vine and the branches, the mustard seed, the tree that will not bear, the seed that falls on rocky ground. We have the imagery of Our Lady as the walled garden and the mystical rose, as well as the mental picture of the Garden of Eden, the fruitful and peaceful home of our first parents before the fall. The parables and comparisons surround one in the garden, and meditation comes easily.

I am happy to know that Tim had his own time in our gardens in Rhode Island, West Virginia, and Massachusetts. He too had the opportunity to absorb the beauty and images of God inherent in each leaf and petal. I remember them with delight as I tend the plants. My greatest happiness, though, rests in the abundance he now shares with the Master Gardener, Creator of all the growing beauty that surrounds us. My heart sings the Te Deum while with grass stained knees and grubby hands I work away.

> *You are God: we praise You;*
> *You are the Lord; we acclaim You;*
> *You are the eternal Father:*
> *All creation worships You.*

The answer created things give to the soul (which interrogates them by reflecting on them) is, as St. Augustine declares, the testimony that they in themselves give the soul of God's grandeur and excellence. God created all things with remarkable ease and brevity, and in them He left some trace of who He is, not only in giving all things being from nothing, but even by endowing them with innumerable graces and qualities, making them beautiful in a wonderful order and unfailing dependence on one another. All of this He did through His own Wisdom, the Word, His only begotten Son by whom He created them.

—St. John of the Cross, *Spiritual Canticle*

August 8, 2006

The dewy grass soaks my sneakers this morning as I go about watering the gardens, a pleasant chore in the early dawn coolness. I get to make the rounds of the blooming plants and bushes, inspect the buds and leaves, and admire the flowers and fruits. The butterflies are profuse, and a hummingbird changes his flight plan when he sees me with the hose. It's another idyllic morning in the country. Amid my inspections I notice the rose bushes I planted a year ago in the Mary Garden. All three are thriving and full of buds and full-blown blooms in pink, red, and white.

These roses have a special significance. First, they are symbols of Mary, the Mystical Rose, and then too, the pink,

AUGUST

red, and white are representations of the joyful, sorrowful and glorious mysteries of the rosary. They also remind me of the thoughtful generosity of three dear friends, Lee, Laurie, and Audrie, who with their families presented them as gifts at the time of Tim's death.

As a flower grower and arranger, I love all flowers, so with humble gratitude I accepted and admired the many bouquets and baskets given to us at the wake and funeral. At the wake, the somber mood brightened considerably when I saw the three potted rosebushes tied with ribbons and read the card that was placed nearby. The best flower for a gardener is one with roots! Later another friend, Susan, helped me to plant them in the garden.

As I think about these roses, I remember today's saint, Dominic, who spread devotion to the Rosary, which the Blessed Mother gave him in a vision. Dominic used this meditation on the life of Our Lord to teach his contemporaries the basics of their faith.

Andy and I had tried over the years to bring our family together each evening to pray the Rosary. As often happens with children, some evenings were more successful than others. It can be difficult to get everyone gathered and even harder to help them change gears from noisy play to quiet reflection. We always included Tim, even as a baby, in our evening prayers. He went from grasping a child's

large-beaded rosary in his little fist, to teething on it, and then the inevitable swinging it around in the air. As he got older we taught him his prayers, and then began each decade of the Rosary with an explanation.

Tim fidgeted and lost interest quickly, but we persisted. When he was old enough to lead a decade, we had to mentally brace ourselves because it would take a while. He would forget his part or drift off or, as he got older, mumble incoherently. We tried lighting candles to attract his attention, and some years later we found a book with a picture for each Hail Mary of each decade. At one point I even resorted to whispering before each Hail Mary an explanation of the events as they unfolded, sort of a blow-by-blow account. This held his interest well, but I had a hard time keeping it up on a regular basis.

Sometimes we followed the question and answer method for each mystery. One night it went like this:

Dad: The first Joyful Mystery: the angel Gabriel appears to Mary.
Mom: Tim, what did Mary say to the angel Gabriel? (I was fishing for "Yes," her "Fiat.")
Tim: Who are YOU?"

We tried hard not to dissolve into laughter.

We continued amid impatience and frustration as the years went on and Tim became more argumentative. We remembered family members who were sick and problems throughout the world. Sometimes Tim would pray for orphans or a new bike or Ginger, the dog. He remembered

Mrs. Castro and Mrs. Oleksak, his lady friends at church; his skiing buddies; his brothers at college or living far away in Hawaii. He reminded us to pray for his sisters-in-law as each joined the family and his nephews as they came into the world. Sometimes our prayer intentions lasted quite some time as Tim gave little details about the person he was praying for. "I want to pray for Tom in Rome. Of course, he's the holiest one in the family . . . he says the most prayers!"

Now our family rosaries are usually offered by just a group of two, but I can't pray without remembering Tim, and I know when all is said and done that at the end, Mary remembered him too.

Pray for us sinners now and at the hour of our death. Amen.

—The Hail Mary

And I was confident in advising you with assurance to pray the Holy Rosary. Blessed be that monotony of 'Hail Marys' which purifies the monotony of your sins.

—St. Josemaria Escriva, *The Furrow*

August 15, 2006

Rain and fog are pervasive this morning, but the moisture is welcome after the dry days of the past few weeks. The birds are active, and from the window I watch as they hop about on the stone wall. On a sunny day I feel pulled outside to work in the garden, but rainy mornings invite reflection and I am content to sit inside with pen in hand. So many memories bubble to the surface this morning. An incident from this week comes to my mind and lingers there, as if on cue, for further examination.

On Saturday I drove down the hills to one of the valley towns, conveying a drawing to be engraved on Tim's headstone. The artist, my friend Laurie, followed. When we reached our destination we unrolled the vellum sketch for the stonecutter to inspect.

I had approached Laurie earlier in the year to see if she would translate an idea onto paper for the stone. The inspiration came from a book published in 1936, *A Retreat with St. Ignatius in Pictures for Children*. Caryll Houselander, an English artist and mystic, created the detailed black and white drawings which accompanied text by a Jesuit, Fr. Geoffrey Bliss. (Sophia Institute Press reissued the book in 1997 as *My Path to Heaven*.) Inside the covers were a series of images which all include a little Crusader holding a candle, his light of faith, as he makes his way through life on his path to heaven, his true home, and to the God who made him.

Tim and I had "read" the book as a meditation for Lent one year, and he could concentrate on the pictures for long periods because they were full of exquisite detail and thought-provoking images. I wanted Laurie to sketch the Crusader with his candle and sword ascending the stairs to Mother Mary, who waits at the top as the Gate of Heaven, her arms outstretched. Laurie found spare moments in her busy life as mother of five (some of Tim's adopted friends) to prepare the drawing in the double lines needed for the stonecutter. Her talent and vision brought my idea to life.

Apart from Caryll Houselander's drawings, which Tim's eyes devoured, there seems to be a connecting thread between Tim and the English artist with the poetic soul. I first encountered her when I read *The Reed of God*, a slim volume published in 1944. In these meditations on the life of the Blessed Mother, Houselander attempted to make Mary visible to us so that by imitating her we might find the intimacy with God which she enjoyed. My copy is stained and the spine is peeling, but it is one of those treasured possessions which I must keep near.

Several months before Tim's death, I sought out a copy of Caryll's memoir *A Rocking-Horse Catholic* and obtained an old 1955 edition on loan from the Boston Public Library. In it Caryll describes three particular visions or experiences in which she saw the image of Christ in her fellow man. In the final experience, she was riding on a London subway train when she saw Christ in His full humanity and glory in every passenger aboard; all those of the past and future were crowded together aboard the train and all were Christ.

These intense visions colored Caryll's life thereafter, and inspired her to show an empathy and compassion for each person she met, but especially for the mentally disturbed and outcasts of her day.

The connecting thread, or maybe it is a golden chain, that binds Tim to Caryll Houselander in my mind is their shared capacity to see the image of God in all men, even if Tim couldn't have articulated it as Caryll could. His mind and his whole being were wired in such a way that he did not see the disfigurements, disabilities, and mannerisms that often stand in the way of our embracing our fellows with the love of God. Tim only recognized the good and lovable in those he met, and he responded to it with a magnetic force that could literally bowl you over. I am ashamed to say it caused me embarrassment at times, but I have learned a supreme lesson. While his exuberance is not in my nature, I hope his loving response will remain with me interiorly throughout my life.

I am eager to see the gray granite image placed in the small country cemetery that sits between the river and the hills, but at the same time I realize the engraving is only, after all, a passing thing. My true eagerness rests upon the reality it portrays.

She passed the multitude of the angels and saints and came at last to a place of solitude; and here her Son came to her, and He was a King in a robe of rose, and his wounds were jewels that shone; and He crowned her with a great crown set with seven brilliant stars for her life's seven sorrows.

—Caryll Houselander, *The Reed of God*

August 22, 2006
Queenship of Mary

It is another perfect summer day in these hills of home. It reminds me of a line from a favorite hymn: "Mary the dawn, Christ the perfect day." Our human minds, so in need of images to flesh out the infinite, can easily grasp the concept of the perfect day. There is something so eternal and other-worldly about such a day. Maybe it is a fleeting glimpse into the perfection that was Eden and a peek into the bliss of an eternity in God's presence. Our spirits rise to meet the reality.

This perfect day provides a fitting setting for today's jewel of a feast. We honored Mary at Mass and then drove to the cemetery for a blessing of the gravestone. Our grandson, Nicholas, almost three, takes off his sandals and walks barefoot in the cool, wet grass as we gather around for the consoling ritual.

"Unless you become like little children you shall not enter the kingdom of heaven." What is it about a child's essence that we need to recapture in order to behold the face of God? As I watch Nicholas and think about the heart of his Uncle Tim, childlike even at the age of fifteen, I am drawn to reflect upon Tim's innocence and yet again upon the simplicity of his character.

Tim was transparent in his desires and actions; there was no duplicity there. The goodness and love blazed out, and at times the impatience and willfulness too. He lived in the present moment and without concern for the future. Those of us adults who retain these features have learned prudence and self-control to accompany them, but a child with no desire to grow up sees no need to cultivate such extra virtues.

Tim told us once when he was seven, "I don't ever want to change into a grown-up. I always want to be a kid." We probed this idea with him to see what he had in mind. He said he would keep having birthdays until he got to twelve and then he would stop. Although he couldn't actually stop having birthdays, the older Tim had no career goals and didn't want to think about the practical skills he'd need as an adult, such as managing money, writing checks, or filling out a job application. As parents we feared for the child who would never get beyond the simplicity of childhood. I made corrections in my vision of the next twenty years and resigned myself to a future that would always include the care of Tim. God accepted my offering, but He knew otherwise.

In his childlike simplicity, Tim always spoke of Mary as one of his three mothers. First there was his birth mother; then me, his "Mom"; and over and above us was Mary, his mother in heaven. As I look at the carved granite and see the little Crusader making his way up the steps to Mary, the Queen Mother, I rest in God's perfect plan. With confidence, I ask the grace for the rest of us to retain or renew the elements of spiritual childhood which will benefit us in our climb up the mountain.

> *On this mountain the Lord of hosts*
> *Will provide for all peoples*
> *A feast of rich food and choice wines,*
> *Juicy, rich food and pure, choice wines.*
> *On this mountain He will destroy*
> *The veil that veils all peoples,*
> *The web that is woven over all nations;*
> *He will destroy death forever.*
> *The Lord God will wipe away*
> *The tears from all faces;*

> *The reproach of His people He will remove*
> *From the whole earth; for the Lord has spoken.*
> *On that day it will be said:*
> *"Behold our God, to whom we looked to save us!*
> *This is the Lord for whom we looked;*
> *let us rejoice and be glad that He has saved us!"*
> *For the hand of the Lord will rest on this mountain.*

—Isaiah 25: 6-10a

August 28, 2006

Today is cool and overcast, and there is that sense in the air that summer is drawing to a close. I put things to rights in the house and garden, and then with overnight bag in tow I head out to my brother Steve's house in Connecticut. Today is our father's 76th birthday and tomorrow is Stephen's 52nd, so we have plans to celebrate with feasting.

Steve was a much-beloved uncle to Tim, always full of the kind of fun that boys especially thrill in: wrestling, ball games, cards, and pool. He included Tim in the fun along with his own boys, and he took the hugs and incessant conversation with good humor.

After dinner at a restaurant on Long Island Sound, we amble along the ocean boardwalk, gulls swooping overhead.

We pass some old bocce players conversing after a game, dodge a few skaters, and take in the sights and smells of the waterfront.

Our conversation turns to the particular joys of oceanside living and the tranquility that the waves engender. My thoughts move quite naturally to Timothy, who was so proud of being born in Rhode Island, the Ocean State. I hear the words of a song the boys sang to Tim when he was small:

> *Every state in the USA has something it can boast of,*
> *A product that the state produces the most of*
> *Rhode Island is little, but Oh my!*
> *It has a product anyone would buy.*
>
> *Copper comes from Arizona, peaches come from Georgia*
> *And lobsters come from Maine.*
> *The wheat fields are the sweet fields of Nebraska*
> *And Kansas gets bonanzas from the grain.*
>
> *Old whiskey comes from Old Kentucky*
> *Ain't the country lucky, New Jersey gives us glue.*
> *And you, you come from Rhode Island,*
> *And little Old Rhode Island is famous for you.*

—Howard Dietz and Arthur Schwartz
"Rhode Island is Famous for You"

AUGUST

After we moved away from Rhode Island, Tim repeatedly begged for a return to the ocean. He loved the waves, the sand, the shells, the strong winds, and the people he would meet. The only thing he didn't like about a trip to the beach was having to pack up and leave. Besides the Rhode Island beaches, Cape Cod was a favorite spot, and he had a chance to experience the Gulf Coast ocean beaches when we traveled to Alabama. His delight buoyed the spirits of the rest of us and his discovery of the ebb and flow of the tides was priceless. Tim found his shadow on a beach, and then there were the pleasures of digging in the sand.

A perfect day at the seaside offers a heightened degree of perfection, for added to the limitless blue sky is the seemingly endless expanse of rolling water. Sight and hearing participate in the perfection, and then the wind and spray enliven our sense of touch. God is present in these experiences of eternity and perfection, and I revel in memory with Tim. Together we thank God for the beauty and the immensity, and for the glimpse of His majesty that the ocean provides.

I stroll along in time with my family, but in spirit I am running and screaming with Tim as he chases the waves and the gulls. May God always lead our memories and imaginations to ponder the workings of His creation and to marvel at His Being.

Ring out your joy to the Lord, O you just;
For praise is fitting for loyal hearts.

Give thanks to the Lord upon the harp,
With a ten-stringed lute sing Him songs.
O sing Him a song that is new,
Play loudly, with all your skill.

For the word of the Lord is faithful
And all His works to be trusted.
The Lord loves justice and right
And fills the earth with His love.

By His word the heavens were made,
By the breath of His mouth all the stars.
He collects the waves of the ocean;
He stores up the depths of the sea.

—Psalm 33

September

September 1, 2006

I leave my country solitude for a second time this week, but today my errand is a sad one. I head east towards Boston for a funeral; Steve, a friend of the family, has died at age thirty-six, another victim of mental illness. Armed with prayer, I steel myself for a difficult day, driving to offer my condolences to the family and my petitions to God. I'm going in the place of Steve's friends in Alabama who cannot make the long trip north. God orchestrates the day well for me: I find the church in time, and later I have ample opportunity to console Steve's mom, Carole, after the burial. I am not left without consolations myself during the beautiful Byzantine liturgy and in the conversations that follow.

Steve and Tim shared some happy celebrations together here on earth, and I pray with my heart intent on the theme of the day, "Mercy triumphs over justice," that these two "lost boys" can join together in the celestial celebration of praise to the Good God.

> *Eternal God, in whom mercy is endless,*
> *and the treasury of compassion inexhaustible,*
> *look kindly upon us, that in difficult moments,*
> *we might not despair, nor become despondent,*
> *but with great confidence,*
> *submit ourselves to Your holy will,*
> *which is Love and Mercy Itself.*

—St. Faustina,
Closing Prayer, Chaplet of Divine Mercy

September 4, 2006

It has been a wild late summer weekend that feels more like fall. The wind was howling on Saturday, and Sunday the rain began in earnest only to continue most of the day. The unseasonable weather has been most unwelcome in our little town, for it is Labor Day weekend and that means the Blandford Fair. For close to 140 years the fairgrounds have hosted farmers and gardeners with their animals and produce, and farm wives with their baked goods and quilts and handiwork. In years past there was even horse racing to liven things up. Today the truck and tractor pulls have taken the place of the racing, and from our house I can hear the engines revving up two miles away.

Now on Labor Day itself the wind and rain have moved on, so the fairgoers will have an easier time negotiating the grounds without mud to contend with. All the townspeople seem to have been recruited to volunteer in one way or another. I see friends and neighbors selling tickets at the gate, manning the Boy Scout booth, and in the volunteer fire department trailer hawking berry shortcakes. I have the enviable duty of selling raffle tickets for an exquisite Baltimore Album quilt I had the pleasure to help create. As I sit inside the white New England gazebo and watch the folks pass by, I think about Tim and how much he loved the fair.

We'd start with a ride on the Ferris wheel and he would buy his once-a-year allotment of cotton candy. We could then move on to the livestock buildings, with Tim petting the sheep and goats and calves and bending down to look the chickens and ducks in the eye. I would listen to him pontificate on his barnyard preferences: ducks were nice, but he didn't want chickens because "they stink as bad as the devil's armpits." (I can date that remark from the time adolescence came along with the required parental talks on hygiene.)

Tim and I would then gravitate to the horse show and watch the various events underway from the bleachers, young and old riders competing under the watchful gaze of the judges. Next would come a stroll along the rows of vendors as we made our way towards the Agricultural Hall.

Once there we'd climb the steep stairs to see the baked goods spread out on shelves inside the glass cases, the vegetables displayed on white paper plates, and the pyramid of garden flowers dominating the back wall. We would walk by the quilts hanging above reach and the wood carving, basketry and other handcrafts. Throughout our inspections Tim was an active partner, hugging me when he saw a ribbon on some article of mine and enthusiastically greeting everyone he knew. He always seemed surprised to recognize a familiar face.

I cherish the simple pleasures of living in a small town—you see familiar faces wherever you go. People care about one another and are eager to share the joys and sorrows of their neighbors. We all have a deep-seated need to be truly known, to have our inner self understood and appreciated by those around us.

But even the closest of human relationships often fall short of this knowledge and appreciation. What we often forget is that this need can only be fully met in our relationship with God, the One who made us and knows our most intimate thoughts and secret desires, and yes, our faults and stumblings too.

This year I'll miss Tim's tug on my arm, pulling me from one wonder to the next, but I will rest with quiet peace in the thought that Tim, who was so known and beloved by his friends—both young and old in and around our town—is now with the God who called him into being and who knows and loves him best.

> *Now we see indistinctly, as in a mirror; then we shall see face to face. My knowledge is imperfect now; then I shall know even as I am known. There are in the end three things that last: faith, hope, and love, and the greatest of these is love. Seek eagerly after love.*
>
> —1 Corinthians 13:12-13; 14: 1a

September 9, 2006

The outdoor task I enjoy perhaps the most, aside from tending the flower gardens, is mowing with the small garden tractor. Sitting at leisure, driving around the grassy areas of the yard and then back to the field of weeds and wildflowers, slows down frantic thoughts and opens me up to experience the peace of meditation and prayer. I once heard a comic routine that told the story of a wise man prescribing a ride on the lawn tractor instead of a visit to the psychiatrist. With ear protectors in place and the hum of the motor drowning out all other sounds, the mind can drift along as the machine follows its back and forth path, and there is a decidedly calming effect.

Tim loved to mow also, but for totally different reasons. With a boy's love of engines and still years shy of being able to drive a car, it gave Tim a sense of power and accomplishment. Other tasks were grudgingly performed, but he always jumped at the chance to ride the tractor. I replay a mental picture of Tim gleefully mowing crazy patterns in the grass.

One day this week, atop the tractor with my mind thus occupied in reverie, I glanced at a strip of wildflowers that separates the vegetable and fruit garden from the back field, and I spotted a patch of color I had never seen before. I turned off the engine to get a closer look at an unusual flower I could not identify. It had large, deep purple buds, similar in shape to rose buds but massed in circles around the stalk; whorled leaves surrounded the buds.

Later I pulled out the wildflower guide to try and identify the plant, but I wasn't able to come up with a perfect match. For several days I walked back to check and see if the flower had opened, thinking first of the beauty yet to come, and then that it might help me with identification. Each time, the bud remained closed. Finally, with the help of a friendly gardener at a tag sale and a wildflower book she was selling, I was able to put a name to it. It is a rare plant in our neck of the woods, a member of the Gentian family. What I discovered about this particular cultivar is that the buds never open—they are called the Closed Gentian.

While happy to have finally named the flower, I was disappointed that the unopened bud would never reveal the beauty inside. I knew that beauty would be there, but I would not see it. On subsequent days following my identification, when I passed the spot while sitting and mowing, I thought about how Tim would have loved to have shared my discovery. And then came a further thought: Tim was like the Closed Gentian. He was an unusual child but beautiful according to the design of his Maker. In retrospect, I see now the exquisite bud that could never open.

When he was younger we had hoped that maturity would solve some of Tim's problems, that he would outgrow them or learn a measure of self-control. We had waited to see how Tim would "open."

In the beginning, it is sad to realize that a child of yours will never fulfill your expectations for him. For us, though, with the help of God's grace came acceptance, and later trust that even if we couldn't envision the future for Tim, God had a plan in mind from and for all eternity. This trust never diminished for me, even after Tim's tragedy of a death, for I clung still more tightly to His mercy and love for the simple, little ones.

It turns out that the closed gentian *is* a perfect specimen—a ripe bud of purple-blue that has reached its maturity of form. I praise God for the created wonders which spring forth from His word, and for the grace to see and accept them for what they are: perfect gifts coming from His bounteous hands.

> *There's not a plant or flower below,*
> *But makes Your glories known;*
> *And clouds arise and tempests blow*
> *By order from Your throne.*
> *While all that borrows life from You*
> *Is ever in Your care,*
> *And everywhere that man can be,*
> *You, God, are present there.*

—Isaac Watts,
"I Sing the Mighty Power of God"

September 14 - 15, 2006
Exaltation of the Cross
Our Lady of Sorrows

Triumph and sorrow. It is hard to imagine the two together in one thought or breath, and yet in this world of ours the sorrow and the pain must always precede the glory and the exaltation. These thoughts are undercurrents swirling below my conscious musings on these two great feasts.

My car is laid up for repairs and after several days of forced retirement on our country estate, I bring Andy to work in the truck so I can get to morning Mass.

We celebrate the triumph of the cross at every Mass but most especially on this feast day in September. As I meditate on the sufferings of Christ, sufferings prompted by a love which knows no bounds, I continuously return to the times which have been most sorrowful for our family.

Archbishop Fulton Sheen said, "In every trial there is the visage of the cross." As we shoulder our own trials with love and faith, we share in the suffering of Christ and in its value. I can see our family on the occasions when the cross was placed squarely before us: Andy's cancer, Paul's tumor, and now still so fresh, Tim's death. I think especially of the mental suffering that Tim endured, a suffering which Caryll

Houselander called "The mind of Christ bleeding under the crown of thorns."

If we can but hold on and unite our sufferings to those of Christ on the cross, we will soon share in the glory that awaits the faithful soul. And what glory awaits the faithful soul! Our pastor reminded us today of the words of St. Peter Julian Eymard: "Divine love always enters the heart through a fresh wound." If God's love can so penetrate our hearts in this earthly life, dare we imagine the beauty of its fulfillment in eternity?

The Church has fittingly placed the feast of Our Lady of Sorrows on the day following the Triumph of the Cross so that we can ponder the love and suffering our dear Mother poured into our redemption. As one totally united to her divine Son, how could she not suffer as He suffered? Mary, too, has won us the salvation that awaits us at the end of our "mourning and weeping in this valley of tears." I unite my own sorrow over the loss of Tim with her unimaginable sorrow, and I gain comfort from her support and her embrace of love.

> *The cross is a shield against the devil as well as a trophy of victory. It is the promise that we will not be overcome by the Angel of Death (Exodus 9:12). The Cross is God's instrument to lift up those who have fallen and to support those still*

on their feet fighting. It is a crutch for the crippled and a guide for the wayward. It is our constant goal as we advance, the very wellspring of our body and soul. It drives away all evils, annihilates sin and draws down for us abundant goods. This is indeed the seed of the Resurrection and the tree of eternal life.

—St. John Damascene, *De Fide Ortodoxa*

She continues to be the loving consoler in the many physical and moral sufferings that afflict and torment humanity. She knows our sorrows well, because she too suffered from the time of Bethlehem until Calvary: 'And a sword will pierce your own soul too' (Luke 2:35). From Jesus on the Cross she has the specific mission only and always to love us in order to save us. Mary consoles us above all by pointing out to us Christ Crucified and paradise. O Consoling Mother, comfort us all, make us understand that the secret of happiness lies in goodness and in always following your Son Jesus.

—Blessed John Paul II, Address, 13 April 1980

September 19, 2006

It's foggy and cool this morning and it feels like it could rain soon, so I hurry to take in the sheets from the clothesline.

Then so it won't get wet, I haul under cover a large piece of a young maple tree I had cut this week. Andy is thinking of using it to make a latch for the barn door and it needs to dry out first.

Another quiet September morning has arrived. The lazy summer days are gone, and the cool weather coupled with the shortening of the evening light spur us on to finish up the outside work before the cold and snow come to stay. Andy is in a rush to finish the siding on the barn and to get the doors made, and I have all the fall chores in the garden. There were lots of windfall peaches yesterday and some raspberries to pick and strawberries to plant.

In the past, my September days were of a decidedly different character. Homeschooling began in earnest after weeks of planning in the summer, and Tim and I were forced to ignore the bucolic scenes outdoors in favor of books and papers and pens. I paged through his portfolio this morning and read some of his compositions from past years.

Tim had a creative mind and an unusual way of using words to express himself. He would change word order around or try out some of his vocabulary words in a new way or make an attempt to interject humor into a paragraph. Getting to the finished product was a long and tedious process, though, due to his problems focusing his attention, his inability to remember letter formation, and a similar problem he had when using a computer keyboard.

So our customary procedure was for me to introduce the topic, and then with pen and paper in my hand I would take down the sentences as Tim dictated them. He would get distracted and I would have to prod him to keep him on task. I'd pose a question or suggest a beginning for a sentence and off he'd go for a while, until the next distraction interrupted him. The cat might jump up on his lap, or the ticking of the clock would disrupt his half-hearted concentration. After I had decided he had composed enough, I would give Tim a break before the next phase of his ordeal was to begin.

When I was sure my handwriting was legible, Tim would sit down in front of the computer and get ready to type up the paper. "Get ready" usually meant half an hour while he chose a font and ink color—the more outlandish the better, in his mind. The actual typing would span the course of several days and involve much complaining and distraction on his part and much cajoling and insisting on mine. We would heave a collective sigh of relief when the printer finally sprang into action.

Looking back over the papers I set aside for his required school portfolio, I am happy to have a record of his thoughts and words. Just as we treasure the many photographs, so too I cherish the papers and drawings. I can read again his composition explaining how to teach a blind person to ski, listen to his excited "Account of my First Flight," read the report of a favorite book we shared aloud, and remember a trip to the Shelburne Museum with his grandparents. All the quirky word usages that are so "Tim" invoke a mental image that is at once real and representative.

I sent a copy of one of his papers out with our Christmas cards last year. It was written when Tim was thirteen, after we had finished the final book of C. S. Lewis' Narnia Chronicles, *The Last Battle*. A short assignment, I asked him to think about the following quotation:

"Yes," said Queen Lucy. "In our world, too, a stable once had something inside it that was bigger than our whole world." I asked him, "What does Lucy mean?"

Here is Tim's response:

> In our world in a stable a child was born, but not just any child—he was God! That child, whose name was Jesus, was smaller in size than the world, but in spirit he was bigger than the universe because he was God and he made the universe! It sounds ridiculous but it happened, and he was so great he became famous for his love and his knowledge and his piety. And that's what Lucy meant.

On the front of the Christmas card was a photograph of a 3-year-old Tim sitting in front of a Nativity set with all the figures lined up facing him. He is clutching Baby Jesus to his heart and smiling with innocent delight as I look on in rapt wonder. My friend Dale calls it "a fine and lasting icon."

No one has ever seen God.
Yet if we love one another
God dwells in us,
And His love is brought to perfection in us.
The way we know we remain in Him
And He in us
Is that He has given us of His Spirit.
We have seen for ourselves, and can testify,
That the Father has sent the Son as Savior of the world.
When anyone acknowledges that Jesus is the Son of God,
God dwells in him,
And he in God.

—1 John 4: 12-15

September 26, 2006

I woke up early this morning to get a jump on the day's work. With my hands in the soap suds I washed up a few dishes and gazed out into the darkness. The sky showed the promise of light near the horizon, so daylight would not be far off. I scrubbed to get a label off a glass bottle and recalled memories of Tim at the sink.

Washing dishes was one of the earliest tasks we set Tim to work at. His desire to "help out" quickly dissolved into a game of pouring and sloshing and flying bubbles. Most children outgrow the impulse to play instead of wash in order to get the job finished quickly, but Tim had a hard time seeing beyond the present and always entered deeply into the fun of the moment—no matter what work was at hand.

Once we were getting ready to make oatmeal cookies together and had assembled all of the ingredients on the kitchen counter. I left the room for a minute. When I came back I discovered that Tim had taken all of the tins, containers, and boxes and made a tower out of them that was taller than he was. His delight in having surprised me was clearly evident, so I played along and brought out the camera before we finally got down to the business of baking. The photo remains another treasure in the family archives.

On another occasion Tim began stringing wooden beads from a basket I kept on hand for visiting little ones. They were many-colored of all shapes and sizes. Before long Tim came proudly to present me with four long necklaces and an empty bead basket. I wear one of these priceless strings from time to time, and whenever I put it on the memories of Tim are strung alongside the circles of wood.

We all need the grace to live in the present moment. For Tim, it was a symptom of his mental illness that he couldn't get beyond the present to consider the future. For those of us more fortunate, it must be a conscious act of the will that

keeps us anchored to the task at hand with the grace God gives at that instant. We put our hands and minds and souls at His disposal and submit to His guidance while resting in His will and love.

> *And so the sequel to the New Testament is being written now, by action and suffering. Saintly souls are in the succession of the prophets and the Apostles, not by writing canonical books, but by continuing the history of divine purpose with their lives, whose moments are so many syllables and sentences through which it is vividly expressed. The books the Holy Spirit is writing are living, and every soul is a volume in which the divine author makes a true revelation of His word, explaining it to every heart, unfolding it in every moment.*
>
> —Jean-Pierre de Caussade,
> *The Sacrament of the Present Moment*

Lots of my present moments are now spent working or driving alone, and I have as much quiet as I desire to ponder God's mysterious ways at each moment and twist and turn of life's journey. Quite a few of these moments are spent pondering Tim's present which is now lived in front of the Divine Presence, a present which will last an eternity. I pray that the syllables and sentences of Tim's short life will inspire us also to live lives that will be, in the words of Father

Caussade, "continuing the history of divine purpose." May we too live close to God in every one of the hundreds or thousands or millions of present moments we have left.

October

October 3, 2006

Yesterday afternoon was sunny and crisply clear, and I walked around the garden checking to see what was in bloom. It is my turn to arrange the flowers to adorn the parish altar this weekend, and I needed to take inventory to see what flowers might be ready to pick. The first frost of the season could come any day now, and I must be vigilant if I want to have any flowers left for Saturday. I was thinking about which annuals and tender perennials I could cut early as I got tarps ready to cover the fall raspberries.

Walking to the back of the garden shed where I would close the shutters to keep out the cold air, I was startled by a sudden flapping of wings. Regaining my composure, I realized that a bat had been hiding out behind one of the shutters. It settled on the shed wall upside down, its furry body heaving and silky wings folded. I had a chance then to study the little finely-formed bat and was not at all repulsed. Bats are helpful in the garden for the quantity of insects they consume, and they are a familiar sight in the evenings as they swoop and glide about, but glimpsing one in the daylight is rare.

Seeing the bat reminded me of a dusky midsummer evening a few years back. Tim was heading out to sleep in a tent he'd pitched in the back field with Michael, a young friend from New York City. Michael was staying with us for several weeks as part of a program that pairs inner city kids with families outside of their crowded urban environments. As the two boys walked back with flashlights and sleeping bags, they encountered a number of bats. Michael was clearly afraid of whatever was flying around him, and Tim was doing his best to calm Michael's fears. Bats were not on Tim's "fear list" along with the moths and dead flies, their absence being one of those inexplicable facets of his phobias. That summer Tim also had to convince Michael that there were no sharks in the little placid country pond we swam in. It was an interesting visit!

I was proud of Tim that summer for his ability to make our guest feel at home. Michael had a different skin color, a different upbringing, a different age and experience, but in Tim's simplicity of mind and heart Michael was just a boy to have fun with. Tim was good at seeing beyond the externals, or maybe he just didn't notice them in his eagerness to love.

Just as Tim had responded as a toddler in West Virginia to the old fellow from the hills, he continued to respond with love and a total lack of prejudice to whomever he encountered as he grew in years. He reached out in friendship to John, the bachelor professor he met at church; Lisë, the babysitter down the road; and Kathy, the UPS driver who dropped off our packages. Tim was ready and eager to call anyone "friend," and in typical extrovert fashion, he didn't wait for an overture from the other party. God surely had a sense of humor in placing him with two introverted parents!

I marvel again at the all-knowing Providence that brought Tim to our family, and I give thanks for the lessons Tim has taught us. Through our many missteps, we need to keep reading the book of his life.

We have to behave as God's children towards all of God's sons and daughters. Our love has to be a dedicated love, practiced every day and made up of a thousand little details of understanding, hidden sacrifice and unnoticed self-giving. This is the good "fragrance of Christ" that made those who lived among our first brothers in the faith exclaim: "See how they love one another!"

—St. Josemaria Escriva,
Christ is Passing By

October 9, 2006

I'm on my knees in the garden again, this time for a necessary but sometimes overwhelming task—weeding. In the quiet outside with only birds and crickets breaking the silence, my thoughts gather round for inspection. Weeding makes me think about pulling out the bad habits and attachments that choke the heart and soul from loving properly, loving God first, and then His children.

Sometimes a weed comes out easily, but when I look closely, I realize I haven't gotten the whole root. There might be part of a tap root left, or perhaps a whole system of smaller root branches and hairs remains behind to put out leaves. So diligence and thoroughness are required in the beginning, and then perseverance with a sharp trowel or hoe even after I'm sure I've pulled out the whole culprit beneath the soil.

I think about those things to which I am attached and those faults that are so stubbornly clinging to me. Most of them are underground, hidden from view. Tim's attachments, on the other hand, were so obvious—right out there in plain sight and proclaimed in bold letters with marquee lights. If you asked him, he would tell you proudly that he wanted to live on cereal and junk food and sweets, spend his life in a messy room, and watch cartoons all day. Our lives were kept busy feeding him nutritious food, teaching him to clean up his messes, finding ways for him to be helpful, and severely limiting the televised junk food.

Given his temperament and mental disabilities, there were bound to be battles. These were many and intense, especially as he got older. I put them behind me and out of mind now. Thanks to a loving God and His sacrifices for our sins, Tim's struggles can now be part of his past and not worth the time for a backward glance.

I can learn from them, though. From watching Tim and his obvious attachments over the years, I recognized that I had my own set of deep-rooted weeds, only I managed to conceal and camouflage them pretty successfully. Sometimes I made half-hearted attempts to pull them out but the roots remained, biding their time until they were ready to send out new shoots. As any gardener knows, it's really a constant life-long struggle, but in the spiritual life there is the promise of God's grace which makes even the most difficult weeding a successful battle. So now, armed with this grace and with Tim's help too, I'll keep hoeing.

> *I can do all things through
> Christ who strengthens me.*
>
> —Philippians 4:13

October 16, 2006

On the drive down the hill to Mass this morning I had a strong auditory memory of Tim. He was sitting in the car on the seat next to me and we were following the same route I am driving today, with the same destination. Tim had brought his brown plastic recorder, and he was playing it as we drove along. Actually, he was trying to figure out the fingering for "Let All Mortal Flesh Keep Silence," that ancient and haunting melody. What a joy that the memory can retain sounds as well as images from the past.

From the time he was a baby, music moved Tim deeply. He was calmed by our singing and humming, and as a toddler he loved a little collection of songs that we played on the tape recorder for him. It was a simple tape sung by a group of mothers harmonizing short songs for the very young. When he was hard to settle at night, I would walk him as I sang them one after another.

> *The sun it rises in the day,*
> *And in the evening slips away.*
> *The moon it rises in the night,*
> *And fades away with the morning light.*
>
> —Waldorf School Mothers' Songs

As Tim got older he sang to himself as he went about his play, and then he tried to join in the singing at church. That's when the "Alleluia" started to be one of his regular choruses. He loved listening to others sing, too. When he was three, his brothers Matt and Tom attended the Trivium School where music was a big part of the curriculum. Tim sat enthralled during the all-school concerts and musical evenings both at school and at home.

He strummed a mandolin and tried to figure out a harmonica, and then the recorder, and later pan-pipes. He did unusual things with the instruments, such as trying to play two recorders at once. He loved to plop himself down in front of a piano to "play." Well before we attempted lessons for our rambunctious boy, he exhibited a compelling curiosity about any and all musical instruments. When we took him to concerts, he raced down afterwards to see if he could get a patient adult to let him try to play the instruments on stage. I can see him now at the Springfield Symphony Hall surrounded by the drums and cymbals and xylophone of the Air Force Band, and just one such patient adult. A church we attended in our travels had a large organ on the main floor, and after Mass Tim was at the side of the willing organist getting a private concert.

He played around on the keyboard at home for a while, and then we finally decided to try and find the right teacher for Tim. Our first attempt was an older lady who didn't have the patience and stamina to put up with his attention problems, movement, and tics. Then we found Catherine, whose musicality and training with disabled and autistic children were a perfect fit. She coaxed music out of Tim, got him to use his despised left hand, and put up graciously but firmly with all his idiosyncrasies. She found Tim a piano to replace the keyboard he usually played on, and Tim loved the resonance and tone of the instrument. He had a good ear and would play to himself when the spirit moved him, but he lacked the perseverance to practice his required pieces for very long.

As the years passed, music still helped Tim settle down at bedtime, and we finally figured out that a tape recorder next to his bed would make all of our lives a lot easier. He had an incongruous collection of favorites: classical harp, ocean waves and the sounds of calling loons mixed with classical piano, Zamfir the pan flutist, a tape from his brother Tom of "The Dissipated Eight"—a group of college students singing and harmonizing a cappella. There were songs of the Erie Canal, Christmas carols any time of the year, early American folk songs, and tunes from the Old West. As we realized music's importance to Tim's moods, we made sure a trip of any duration was accompanied by several tapes.

OCTOBER

Catherine sang at Tim's funeral as her husband Tim accompanied her on the organ. Later we were consoled by the harmonizing voices at the graveside, and cheered at home afterward by the sounds of fiddle and guitar. Music was there at his beginning and at his end. And as music had soothed Tim, so we too were caught up in its embrace of beauty. As for Tim, he now hears the music of the spheres. His love of music is completely satisfied as he joins in with the angelic beings and purified souls singing unending praise to the Trinity.

> *Let all mortal flesh keep silence*
> *And with fear and trembling stand;*
> *Ponder nothing earthly minded,*
> *For with blessing in His hand*
> *Christ our Lord to earth descends now,*
> *Our full homage to demand.*
>
> *Rank on rank the host of heaven*
> *Spreads its vanguard on the way,*
> *As the Light of Light descends now*
> *From the realms of endless day,*
> *That the powers of hell may vanish*
> *As the darkness clears away.*

—Liturgy of St. James, 5th Century

October 24, 2006

This morning finds me in scarf and gloves contemplating the sunrise over the ocean in Rye, New Hampshire instead of the view over our foggy hills of home. I am blessed with the chance to vacation for several days with my mother, and we dress hurriedly in the morning darkness and head for the beach. When we arrive the sky is just beginning to color: tufts of cotton candy pink amid the gray blue sky. As the color intensifies, the orange ball of the sun suddenly appears in a blast of color and light. For a few minutes it shines forth brilliantly and casts an orange glow upon the waves before being obscured again behind the steely clouds.

I think of Tim and the clear brightness of his moments of insight that would suddenly burst forth in blazing glory, only to be overshadowed quickly by the grim reality of his mental disorder. Looking back, I remember that many of these epiphanies occurred during Mass, and I can only thank God that I was granted the privilege to observe these movements of grace in his soul.

Once when he was returning to his pew after receiving Holy Communion, he leaned over and said, "Mom, I taste something sweet. I think it's the Holy Spirit!" We were able to witness many such transforming moments in Tim's life, and we stored them away in memory as a defense against the dark times.

> *The ends of the earth stand in awe*
> *At the sight of your wonders.*
> *The lands of sunrise and sunset*
> *You fill with your joy.*

—Psalm 65

Tim has reached the land of sunrise and sunset and is now bathed in light and clarity, and we too receive the sweetness of heavenly consolations. In all things and in all times may God be praised!

October 31, 2006

Our property here in the hills was once pasture land for a cattle ranch, so many of the trees had long ago been felled, but forests border the house and fields on all sides. There are lots of white pine and hemlock, maple, oak, birch, and beech. Nearby is a state forest, too, so trees are an ever-present feature of our landscape hereabouts.

For a family of boys, it was a place of limitless tree-climbing possibilities. Tim was four when we moved here and climbing was already a part of his being. He liked the action of climbing, and he liked the heights he could achieve. I learned to look away lest I let my mother-fears get in the way of his adventures.

There are a number of trees I have come to love on our home ground. One is the climbing tree right outside the window where I am writing. It is a medium-sized maple tree whose former owners left the low horizontal branches intact, so they are perfect to hang onto and pull up from into the higher branches. This was Tim's favorite tree to climb. He watched birds from up in its limbs, called to us to wave as we were working in the yard, and hollered farewell to visiting guests as he looked out from the top branches over the house. His brothers and friends and nephews were his partners in tree climbing, and when none of them were around he tried to entice me to join him. "Come on, Mom. You remember how to climb trees, don't you?"

After his funeral the tree was the centerpiece for our celebration of Tim's life, and it was crawling with young friends and cousins. At one point I looked up and observed a grandfather and an uncle too.

Then there's the ash tree on the far side of the driveway. Andy tied a wooden-seated swing to a branch about twenty feet up, and the seat had the amazing property of spinning as well as swinging anyone who hopped aboard. This was a favorite spot for Tim, who seemed to be soothed by the frantic spinning and developed lots of strategies for attaining the highest arc possible in a straight swing.

Today the ash tree and a fifty foot white pine, which had stood proudly in the center of our circular driveway, were felled, both casualties of last summer's barn fire. Because I am fond of venerable old trees and attached to these particular ones—both fixtures of our landscape and beloved by Tim—it was hard to see them come down. I had an assignment from Andy to record it all on film, so I braced myself and tried to enjoy the beauty of the warm October day.

As God arranged it, the actual event was easier to bear than my fears anticipated. (A lesson here, I am sure, that needs learning over and over again.) The tree man we had contracted, recommended by a friend in town, brought his two oldest daughters along to help with the clean-up. I got them to try out the marvelous swing for one last voyage before the great ash came down. Their friendly presence, added to the fine skill of their father as he brought the giants down with well-placed thuds, brought a fitness to the day. Tim must have liked knowing that some other home-schooled kids had one last swing on the old tree and were the ones who raked and piled the branches.

Our lives are not the same without Tim and now the landscape reflects this change. Only the stumps remain to remind us of the trees that had once grown there. But just as we use the firewood and hardwood boards and wood chips that were once living things, so we use the lessons our life with Tim has taught us. We benefit from the graces that have come to us because we cherished him, and now we benefit too from the great grace of having one of our own to intercede for us with our Creator. In the cycles of life and the economy of salvation, nothing is ever wasted.

> *Every happening, great or small, is a parable whereby God speaks to us, and the art of life is to get the message.*
>
> —Malcolm Muggeridge

November

November 1, 2006

Today and tomorrow are days particularly dear to me. While we have many exalted feast days in the liturgical year, days to remember lofty saints and seasons of solemn repentance, expectation, and jubilation, sometimes these can seem far removed from our daily, ordinary lives. But on All Saints Day, we ponder once again the truth that sanctity is for each of us, no matter our station in life.

We also ponder the strong connectedness to our brothers and sisters in time, and out of time, through the Communion of Saints. We on earth, the Church Militant, remember those members of the Church Triumphant who have reached their eternal destination of bliss and are counted now among the saints in heaven. So many led unremarkable lives and yet through their heroic love achieved a place near Our Lord.

Living on a dirt road that goes nowhere, two miles from the center of our little town, it has been easy to distance ourselves from the riotous revelry of the All Hallows' Eve and to concentrate more on the All Hallows. We didn't forbid Tim the childish fun of door to door trick-or-treating in costume, but since we had to drive somewhere to begin the traditional tramp, and since no children ever came as far as our house to beg candy, we made All Saints Day our main focus instead. There were lots of ways to be creative in finding costumes to portray a particular saint, and lots of saints to appeal to little boys. Our circle of families always had an event or two from which to choose.

The November after Tim's death, a young friend of his named Michael wanted to dress up as Tim for the All Saints Party. "Well," he reasoned to his mother, Audrie, "he *is* in heaven now!" Audrie commended Michael for his idea but told him she was afraid it would bring tears to too many eyes. O, the simple faith of the little ones!

The yearly All Saints' celebration was just the icing on the cake for our family, though, because every day had its own special saints whom we learned about as the calendar brought them to our attention. St. Joseph, St. Nicholas, and the Blessed Mother had festive celebrations, as we enjoyed their days' own foods and traditions. Then there were the patrons of family members who got top billing when their feasts rolled around. When it was his turn, Tim got to celebrate the feasts of St. Timothy in January, and with his dad,

St. Andrew in November, and after his Confirmation, St. Zozimus in late March. The guest of honor helped choose the menu and received small tokens of esteem from the family, but the most solemn tradition was the celebration of Mass, and at home, petitions for the holy one's blessing upon their namesake.

What a comfort to know we have a band of brothers praying for us and inspiring us to keep running the good race and fighting the good fight.

Monsignor Ronald Knox preached in his All Saints Day sermon of 1950:

The light of their example shines down on us, and makes it easier sometimes, to see what we ought to do. They can help us with their prayers, strong prayers, wise prayers, when ours are so feeble and so blind. When you look out on a November evening, and see the sky all studded with stars, think of those innumerable saints in heaven, all ready to help you.

On this chill November night, that gaze up at the heavens brings to mind names of loved ones dear to us . . . our grandparents, saintly priests we have known, elderly friends whose long suffering example was so edifying and young ones brave in their acceptance of misery, Andy's father Joseph. And now our own Tim, whose love and innocence and simple faith have caught the eye and merciful gaze of

His Father God. We beg our son's help as we plod on here below, and we ask for the gift to "become as little children" in our own love of God and charity toward neighbors.

> *O blest communion, fellowship divine!*
> *We feebly struggle, they in glory shine;*
> *Yet all are one in Thee for all are Thine:*
> *Alleluia! Alleluia!*
>
> *But, lo! there breaks a yet more glorious day;*
> *The saints triumphant rise in bright array;*
> *The King of glory passes on His way:*
> *Alleluia! Alleluia!*

—William Walsham How,
"For All the Saints"

November 2, 2006

It was rainy today, and so in the gray drizzle I drove past the cemetery where we usually celebrate our All Souls Day Mass, and over the green bridge to the church. I thought about the countless other Catholics assembling in cemeteries and churches throughout the world to pray for the dead. Joined as we are in charity to our brothers and sisters, we do not forget those in the Church Suffering—those souls who are now being purified in purgatory from the stain of sin, near to perfect union with God but not there yet. We remember them especially today and throughout the month of November.

Tim learned to pray for these departed friends when he was still quite young. Before and after every meal we added to our grace the Church's prayer: "May the souls of the faithful departed, through the mercy of God, rest in peace. Amen." This beautiful tradition has a special history in our family; the practice was begun decades ago after my mother's grandmother died. When we listed our intentions before the nightly rosary and again before bed, Tim often remembered those he knew who had died: his grandfather Joseph, his friend John, and Pope John Paul II.

Although we have a strong certainty, based on his simplicity of soul and his handicapped will, that Tim has himself now made that transition from purgatory to heaven, we continue to pray for him and have Masses said for the repose of his soul. What good parent would refuse to comfort his child when there is even a chance he is in need of assistance?

Tim was always the one ready at hand with love and compassion. He was ever on the lookout for any orphans who were lost and wandering and could come and live with us. Now I have a mother's strong sense, a kind of spiritual intuition, that Tim is inspiring us to pray for the forgotten souls, the "orphan souls" who have been abandoned in prayer by their families and friends. The boy I taught to pray returns the favor, teaching me to pray for Purgatory's spiritual orphans. The sooner we on earth speed them into heaven, the sooner Tim can welcome his many friends into their Father's house.

> Eternal rest grant unto them, O Lord,
> And let perpetual light shine upon them.

It is therefore a holy and wholesome thought
To pray for the dead
That they may be loosed from their sins.

—2 Maccabees 12:44

The holy souls in Purgatory. Out of charity, out of justice, and out of excusable selfishness (they have such power with God!) remember them often in your sacrifices and in your prayers. May you be able to say when you speak of them, 'My good friends, the souls in Purgatory.'

—St. Josemaria Escriva,
The Way

NOVEMBER

November 7, 2006

I walked out to the road to get the mail in the early evening and it was already dark. It's hard to get used to the end of Daylight Savings Time. My heightened senses reverberated with the crunch of dry leaves and gravel in the driveway and the smell of wood smoke, leaf mold, pine needles, and sawdust.

I think about the sense of smell as I walk towards the light of the house and open the door to the warm fragrance of bread baking and spaghetti sauce bubbling on the stove. These are basic, nurturing smells, and I wonder at the feelings they arouse in my being.

Maybe something similar prompted Tim to fantasize about the "giant bread bed." He loved homemade bread, and his well-developed sense of smell always told him when there was a loaf or a pan of rolls in the oven. One day he concocted an outlandish scheme that had us laughing at its scope and particulars.

Tim said he loved the smell of baking bread so much that he wanted to find a baker who would make a giant loaf of bread for him. He then described, with matchless detail, how he would get a huge knife to cut off the top and then scoop out the insides so it would be large enough for him to lie down in. At bedtime, he'd climb in, and then we would carefully put the top of the loaf back on and he could sleep on a soft bed surrounded by the best smell in the world.

Bread is such a basic part of the diet in almost every culture. It is no small wonder Jesus used bread to bring us first an image of our need and His fulfillment—"I am the bread of life, he who comes to me shall not hunger"—and then through His death the gift of His very self in the Eucharist as the food that sustains and delights us.

As I lay the warm, fragrant loaf on the table, I give joyful thanks and praise for this daily bread and for the daily food of my soul, Jesus Christ: body, blood, soul and divinity present under the appearance of bread. "Happy are those who are called to His supper."

> *See how marvelously inventive is our Lord's love!*
> *He alone devised this work of His love.*
> *Who else could have foreseen it, or even dared*
>   *think of it!*
> *. . . It was beyond the angels themselves . . .*
> *"You need bread? I shall be your bread."*
> *And He died happy, because He left us bread,*
>   *and what bread!*
> *His happiness was that of a father who has worked*

NOVEMBER

> *all his life with one purpose in mind: that his
> children might have bread after he was gone.
> What more could the Lord give us?*
>
> —St. Peter Julian Eymard,
> *The Testament of Jesus Christ*

November 8, 2006

The logs from the white pine and the ash tree lie piled on the side of the driveway awaiting the saws. Some of the ash will be cut into firewood, but the larger logs will be cut into boards to await the carpenter's inspiration, while the pine trunk is destined to become planks for the barn walls. My father has a milling attachment for his chain saw and he is eager to begin work so the boards have time to dry out before use.

Andy has gone to work this morning so Dad is busy by himself outside. When the first log is nearly squared off, my mother and I hear the yells and then rush to see Dad clutching his bloody hand. The chainsaw started to fall and several fingers were badly cut as he instinctively reached to grab it. At first Dad is mad at himself for not following his own safety guidelines, but as we near the emergency room he has calmed down, although clearly in pain.

The inevitable waiting begins, and I replay other frantic trips to the ER. I can hear Alex in the backseat after his face has collided with a wooden swing. "Grandma, why did God let this happen to me? I don't want anything bad to happen to God!" I can see Tim's hand wrapped in a bloody towel after he cut his thumb whittling with a new pocket knife. Several years later when he was afraid to look at the scar on his hand, he prayed that God would take him back to the fateful day so he could undo the damage.

We are slow to accept catastrophes and often grumble and rail at God for permitting injuries and accidents and, yes, even deaths. We echo Alex's question: "If God loves me, why would He let this happen?"

The great mystery of suffering can only be understood when we accept the dual reality of God as a God of love and men as creatures of free will. God simply wills the ultimate good for us, but it can only be achieved when we unite our pain and suffering with the pain and agony of Christ on the cross. God loves us enough to permit our purifying trials, and we must love Him enough to accept what comes from His loving hand as the means to our ultimate good.

Hard enough for a five-year-old to understand, but a child's acceptance can sometimes far outstrip our older and supposedly wiser selves.

NOVEMBER

In order to perceive the true answer to the "why" of suffering, we must look to the revelation of divine love, the ultimate source of the meaning of everything that exists. Love is also the richest source of the meaning of suffering, which always remains a mystery: we are conscious of the insufficiency and

inadequacy of our explanations. Christ causes us to enter into the mystery and to discover the "why" of suffering, as far as we are capable of grasping the sublimity of divine love.

—Blessed Pope John Paul II,
Salvifici Doloris

*Turn Your ear, O Lord, and give answer
For I am poor and needy.
Preserve my life, for I am faithful:
Save the servant who trusts in You.*

*You are my God; have mercy on me, Lord,
For I cry to You all the day long.
Give joy to Your servant, O Lord,
For to You I lift up my soul.*

*O Lord, You are good and forgiving,
Full of love to all who call.
Give heed, O Lord, to my prayer
And attend to the sound of my voice.*

*In the day of distress I will call
And surely You will reply.
Among the gods there is none like You, O Lord;
Nor work to compare with Yours.*

All the nations shall come to adore You
And glorify Your name, O Lord:
For You are great and do marvelous deeds,
You who alone are God.

—Psalm 86,
Office for the Dead

November 18, 2006

The wind has been vicious lately. Most of the trees are bare now except for the oak and beech, which hold onto their brown parchment leaves the longest. The fierce winds have saved us the task of raking though, blowing the leaves into the woods and hollows more completely than any noisy machine. Today, however, the wind is gone and there is a palpable calm about the place.

Tim would have been seventeen today, and I carry thoughts of him round about me, pulling them close like a fuzzy, comforting blanket. We remember and pray for him at Mass, along with those who knew Tim and loved him well. We also beg Tim's intercession with God for those of us here below.

Last year on this day, we planted a tree to remember Tim. It was a *syringa reticulata*, a lilac tree, carefully chosen with his cousin Monica's help and hauled, in the back of our truck, up the mountain from the nursery. Tim's Uncle Steve and Aunt Gail and cousins David and Daniel helped us plant it on that chill, blustery November day. We dug the hole behind the apple trees, with the field providing a backdrop of somber brown.

I can see the lilac tree from every back window of the house, and I inspect it whenever I make the rounds on foot or on the tractor. In late spring it bloomed as promised: white spires of heavily-perfumed flowerlets that cheered our souls.

Later today, after a brief visit to the cemetery, Andy and I drive in the gathering dusk beside the river to the vigil Mass where a new child of God, Matthew James Joseph Mary, will be welcomed. Matthew's adoption was finalized yesterday, and the cherubic toddler with the golden curls and frantic squirming is visibly calmed by the cool water poured over his head.

My mother's heart is full of thankfulness at the timing of the event, knowing as I do that there are no coincidences in God's designs. There is a beautiful continuity of life and love in the prayers of Matthew's mother Barb to our son Tim. She begged his help in straightening out the complicated web of pre-adoption tangles which, untangled, have led up to the moment we witness today. Another of Tim's beloved orphans finds a home in this family and in the family of God. Happy Birthday Tim!

> *In Him we were also chosen, destined in accord with the purpose of the One who accomplishes all things according to the intention of His will, so that we might exist for the praise of His glory, we who first hoped in Christ.*

—Ephesians 1: 11-12

November 23, 2006
Thanksgiving

The cat is in from his prowling on this wet night, and Andy and I are home from our Thanksgiving feasting. We are settled companionably on the couch with a pot of tea between us. As I sit and think about the day and its many blessings, I ponder the nature of gratitude.

Thanksgiving is really an action that requires both a giver and a receiver. When we have been blessed with much abundance—a loving family, a bountiful table spread with every manner of succulent food, the health to enjoy it— then it is only a necessary response to thank the host, thank the cook, and thank the Good God from whom we derive these graces and benefits. As we said grace around the table this afternoon, we spoke aloud our gratitude to God for the many gifts we had each received. It was only fitting and proper. We live in a time, however, when lip service is often given to the notion of thanksgiving and God is left out of the picture. People talk about "giving thanks" but forget "to God."

Just as we had taught his older brothers so too we tried to teach Tim at a young age to be grateful to God for each day's blessings. We wanted him to understand that thanksgiving is properly a daily and not just a once a year event. A part of our night prayers together would be a litany of the favors we had received over the course of the day. Tim's thanks would often be for his bicycle, or for his cat, or the cookies Mom had baked for dessert. We treasured these end of the day conversations with God when we had the active Tim safely bedded down for the night and in a reflective mood. They were tender moments.

Tim would have thanked God tonight for the old priest who said Mass this morning, for his friend Mark's tiny dog, Barbie, for the turkey and the pumpkin pie, for the Scrabble game with Baily, for sitting and reading books with his nephew Nicholas, for the bear hug from his Uncle Steve, for the people who were there to wash the dishes so he wouldn't have to.

God is worthy of our thanks and we have been greatly blessed with all manner and number of bounties, both material and spiritual. As I bask in the glow of God's love this night, I recite my own litany and know that my humble prayers of acknowledgement rest in large measure upon the gift of Tim. Deo gratias.

> *Now thank we all our God*
> *With heart and hands and voices,*
> *Who wondrous things hath done,*
> *In whom His world rejoices;*
> *Who from our mothers' arms*
> *Hath blessed us on our way*
> *With countless gifts of love,*
> *And still is ours today.*

—Martin Rinkart,
"Now Thank We All Our God"

December

December 5, 2006

Out the window I can see the snow lying lightly atop the stones on the rock wall. It is falling slowly, and there is that still silence and calm that accompanies a gentle snowfall. Today it feels like December. After a warm November with no sign of snow on the horizon, it is beginning to seem like we actually might progress into winter instead of remaining in a forever fall.

Yesterday I cut the pine boughs and holly branches for the Advent wreath. I am late again this year, and I have even forgotten to buy the purple and rose candles. The circle of evergreen is formed now and I pull out several fresh memories, still green.

I had fashioned another Advent wreath and had suspended it from the ceiling, after the Von Trapp tradition, between the dining room and the living room in our Shrewsbury house. Timothy had just gained his second year and the wreath looked ever so much like a basketball hoop, so that was how he used it when he thought no one was about. The ever-present chronicler of family life caught it on film, however.

Two years later, after a year's sojourn in West Virginia, Advent found us unpacking in the Massachusetts hills. The Advent wreath rested atop the table in the dining room and Tim, now four, was fascinated with the lighting of the candles. His job was to use the candle snuffer to extinguish them at the end of our evening meal. One night, after the house was quiet with everyone asleep (or so we thought), Tim got up for a prowl. He found some matches and thought he would practice lighting candles so that he could have his own turn with the evening ritual.

The result was a fire in the living room, and thankfully a screeching smoke alarm which awoke Andy and me. The little culprit ran away from the scene of the crime unhurt. Several boxes of unpacked books, the arm of the couch, the carpet, and the sooty walls all bore testimony to the deed.

We hugged Tim close and scolded at the same time, but the hugs won out in the end. The attention of the angels and the grace of God had given our parental fears and panic a reprieve: the boy was intact and safe again.

The next evening as we sang "O, Come, O Come Emmanuel" I gave silent thanks for the near escape and rejoiced that we were together to sing another day.

Advent is that beautiful waiting and watching time. In memory and in prayer we relive the expectant days gone by when the world waited and longed for the promised Savior. Our world is so in need of His rebirth in our hearts, of a renewal of our child's faith, of our trust in a Father who fulfills every promise with a bounteous hand.

I will miss Tim's voice when we light the purple candle tonight and try to sing our verses with a sense of real expectation. I will put the matches out of reach from force of habit. The song of my heart will plead with a new pathos.

> *O come, thou Dayspring from on high,*
> *And cheer us by thy drawing nigh;*
> *Disperse the gloomy clouds of night,*
> *And death's dark shadow put to flight.*

I will sing with renewed hope the refrain from "O Come, O Come, Emmanuel," those ever ancient and ever new words, where our longing is met and put to flight by Love.

Rejoice! Rejoice! Emmanuel shall come to thee, O Israel!

December 9, 2006

The days and weeks and months have passed in the blink of an eye, and now the year of remembering has finished its course. I started writing this diary on another cold December day; having come full circle I will lay my pen down this night of cold, clear, crisp stillness lit by brightly shining stars. The memories, the wonder, the gratitude, and yes, the sorrow, I will carry about me always, some as a welcome

cloak on a cold night and the others as a heavy but well-loved cross upon my shoulder.

I have been awed by love during this year of introspection, amazed again by the impact of the life of one human person on the lives of those he touched. I have visited in memory Tim's babyhood, his toddling, running, climbing years. I have heard his voice and read his love notes to me. I've watched him being carried by his brothers and fed by his dad, taught by his grandpas and loved by his grandmas. I have followed behind as he romped with his friends and cousins and nephews. I have cried with him and read to him and been loved fiercely by him and hugged 'til I cried "Uncle." I will go on forever in this life remembering Tim and loving Tim and missing Tim.

And can it be that in a world so full and busy, the loss of one creature makes a void in any heart, so wide and deep that nothing but the width and depth of eternity can fill it up!

—Charles Dickens

And daily I will hear those oft-repeated words:

"Do you love me Mom? Will you always love me? Never stop? Famous words?"

Love is what remains: our love for Tim, his love for us, that big-hearted, extra large, jumbo-sized love. But beyond human love, over and around us is the love of God which surpasses all understanding in depth and strength and tenderness. He brought Tim to us, trusted us to be the guardians of his body and mind and soul, helped us to raise Tim, and at the end supported us in our grief. It was knowing Tim that gave us a glimpse into the essence of God, but it has been losing Tim that truly opened up the heart of Jesus to us.

What a legacy! For gifts such as these we stumble and stutter when we attempt to find words that are worthy enough to express a proper gratitude.

> *I love the Lord for He has heard*
> *The cry of my appeal;*
> *For He turned His ear to me*
> *In the day when I called Him.*
>
> *They surrounded me, the snares of death,*
> *And the anguish of the tomb,*
> *They caught me, sorrow and distress.*
> *I called on the Lord's name.*
> *O Lord my God, deliver me!*
>
> *How gracious is the Lord, and just;*
> *Our God has compassion.*
> *The Lord protects the simple hearts;*
> *I was helpless so He saved me.*

DECEMBER

Turn back, my soul, to your rest
For the Lord has been good;
He has kept my soul from death,
My eyes from tears
And my feet from stumbling.

I will walk in the presence of the Lord
In the land of the living.

—Psalm 116:1-9

Stillness descends upon the house, the ticking of the clock and Andy's rhythmic slumbering breaths, the humming of the refrigerator and the furnace, the purring of the cat stretched out in repose. I keep vigil this night as I draw my thoughts to a close. So I end this year of recorded memory, but of course I will continue remembering until the end of my days. The relics are all about me: the photograph of Tim clapping in delight before the waves, the Waldo book he laughed over, the Daddy he loved. Some catch my eye at unexpected moments—the chewed top of a pen, the tic tac toe scratches on the bed frame, the imprint of golf ball dimples on a wallboard. Some I keep deliberately close by, such as the strands of hair from his last hair cut which I wear in a pocket in my scapular. Each will continue to bring Tim to mind as I go about my days.

It has been a year of Psalms too. From those recited by Pastor Cook the morning of Tim's death to those prayed through my daily recitation of the Divine Office, the psalms have accompanied this journey of days. The mourning psalms, the psalms of praise, the psalms of triumph and gladness, all have helped to bring my soul the blessed peace that can always be found when one rests in the will of God and upon the heart of Christ.

In this wonderful time of Advent hope, my heart sings to God, our "Lord of All Hopefulness" with an Irish melody:

> *Lord of all kindliness, Lord of all grace,*
> *Your hands swift to welcome, Your arms to embrace,*
> *Be there at our homing, and give us, we pray,*
> *Your love in our hearts, Lord, at the end of the day.*

Amen and Alleluia!

Conversations

Spiritual Insights

Fall 1999 and Tim is coming out of the bathroom:

"Mom, God should have made Eve first." (Why, Tim?)

"Because then she could give birth to Adam."

Tim whispers to me during the Stations of the Cross one Lent:

"Mom, I think Jesus was allergic to sin."

During a healing Mass in 2001

At the homily: "This priest is a gift . . . his enthusiasm is a gift."

When told in the homily that since God was our Father and Mary our Mother, we were all sisters and brothers, he turns around to those behind us and says, "You're my sister, you're my brother" and enthusiastically shakes their hands.

During Mass when the pastor is talking about supporting a bill to define marriage as "the union between one man and one woman, not two men and two women."

Tim leans over and whispers to me:

"You COULD have a wedding where two men get married to two women at the same time. You could even have two priests!"

(I am full of joy at his innocent misunderstanding.)

Tim's love of proverbs

The favorites: "Time will tell." "You never know!" "We'll see what happens."

The phone rings and he answers it and discovers it is a wrong number. His advice to the callers:

"Well, you know what they say, 'If at first you don't succeed, try, try again!'"

Word Play

After reading "deer mice" during a science lesson:
"Dear Mice,
Please write back soon!
Love, Tim"

When eating beets: "Beets must be good for your heart." (Why, Tim?)
"You know . . . heartbeats!"

Tim gets his camera and takes a picture of Mom and Dad looking at the atlas.

"It's not the *hilarious* trip anymore, the trip to Alabama is real!"

(He means hypothetical, one of his new vocabulary words.)

Family Moments

I am doing laundry and come up from the basement to discover Tim making a 911 call. His

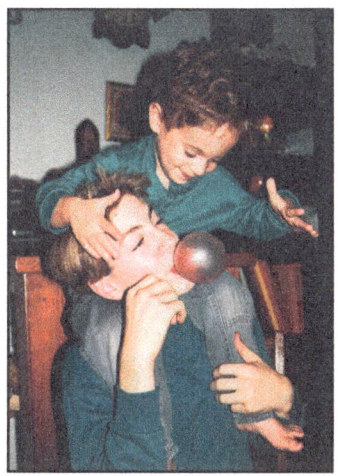

emergency . . . Mom is making him do schoolwork so he can't watch TV!

"I know why Dad likes chocolate lemon donuts . . . he's a little bit sweet and a little bit sour!"

While taking a hike he makes Dad stop on the trail and says,

"You know, Dad . . . we're in the present now and when we get up ahead it's the future. We'll see

some exciting things and have some adventures . . . and behind us is the past."

Upon hearing of his brother Matt's upcoming wedding:

"Do you know what I'm happy about? When Anya moves into our family, we'll have a sister! We need one, don't we? And Anya's the one!"

To his brother Paul's fiancee, Jasmine:
"It would be really nice if you were a Catholic, then we could all go to church together and you'd be part of the community."

Tim cuts up the first draft of Tom's paper for school.

He finds Andy's hammer and starts pounding nails on the stairs.

At the dinner table, age 8:
Dad passes food to Mom by placing dishes on top of the water pitcher.
She says, "Andy, Andy, what are we going to do with you?"
Tim is quiet for a long while and then says, "We could give him to a widow."

After we determine he knows what a widow is, we explain why we can't give Daddy to a widow. More quiet eating . . . then, "There are orphans whose parents have died. We could bring them home to live with us and then we'd have a big family. Do you think there are some of those out there?"

"When I grow up I'm going to have three names: Heater-Lighter, Rock-Climber, Basketball Player."

February 1996, latest complimentary nickname: "You great big hunk of happiness!"

Conversations

Very early:
Andy and Tim in the car . . . Tim is very quiet.
(What are you doing Tim?)
"I'm checking to see if my nails are on the right fingers."
(Are they?)
"Yup."

"I am growing strong brains to think with."

Circa 1996: Someone asks Tim how cars are made.

"The pieces fit together like a puzzle and then they are glued."

(Are they made in a factory?)

"No. God makes them. He's very powerful!"

And from the same era:

"Mom, I just blessed the kerosene heater."

(Did you use holy water?)

"No, I just used my hands. I'm very powerful, you know."

Observation on the way home from a trip to visit the grandparents:

"The tires sound like they are marching on the road."

"I don't want to get rid of my energy. I want to keep it."

When Mom knocks on the bathroom door to hurry him along:
"Just do what I do, Mom . . . Dance around!"

Tim thinks that since Andy works at a hospital (really a nursing home) he is a doctor and can help Anya deliver her baby.

*Dealing with the
signs of mental illness*

(Mom calls Tim to come.)
"I can't now, I'm telling myself a story."
(This goes on audibly for almost an hour.)

Early:
"I'm my own self boss."
Later when grammar sense improves:
"I'm the boss of my life."

I find all the animal photographs off the bathroom walls and question Tim about it.

"They are ugly and staring at me."

Tim starts his obsessive bottle cap collecting. Any dirty old ones will do. Best place to find them is in the church parking lot which borders a liquor store. This is followed by collecting of old junk, preferably of the rusty metal variety.

He and his friend Justin will finance a trip to the Grand Canyon by redeeming cans and bottles for deposit.

The Bedtime Prayer

"Dear God,

If you know of any orphans, guide them to homes where people are to take care of them. If there are any around here (Do you know of any orphans around here, Mom?) send them to our house. Help us find space for them and money to buy their clothes and help the prices of food be low so people could buy food for them. Amen."

For our priests,
to whom we owe so much

Exercises, prayer, and meditation, organized and nationwide, individually or in groups

Start the crusade with a party of one: yourself. This revised and expanded booklet, available in many languages, contains new material, many new photographs to inspire, and hundreds of points and prayers for meditation and reflection before the Blessed Sacrament—all with one goal in mind: to support our beleaguered priests and bishops.

A small sampling of the contents

- New Preface by Cardinal Mauro Piacenza, Prefect of the Congregation for Clergy
- Pope Benedict XVI's memorable 2006 message to priests and deacons during his visit to Germany, one of the world capitals of anti-clericalism
- How do lay women help priests fundamentally, without knowing them? St. Pius X explains and exhorts
- St. Augustine, Pope John Paul II, John Paul I
- The seven most inspiring women of the Church who figure prominently in the theme of spiritual maternity for priests
- "Fifteen Minutes in the Company of Jesus in the Blessed Sacrament," laid out in three succinct pages
- Four prayers recommended ... and the story of a leading bishop who realized he owed his priesthood to the prayers of a stranger, the least and most anonymous nun in a convent

Published with the approval of the Holy See

Roman Catholic Books, P. O. Box 2286, Fort Colllins, CO 80522
BooksforCatholics.com